APPALACHIAN HERITAGE

VOL. 44, NO. 4
FALL 2016

ESTABLISHED IN 1973

PUBLISHED QUARTERLY
by Berea College
CPO 2166
205 N. Main Street
Berea, KY, 40404
www.appalachianheritage.net

 Periodicals postage paid at Berea, Kentucky, and at additional mailing offices. ISSN# 03632318.

 Thanks to Denise Giardina for her gracious permission to reprint "A Mountaintop Experience," which first appeared in the anthology *We All Live Downstream: Writings About Mountaintop Removal* (MotesBooks) and "Mourning in the Mountains," which first appeared in the *New York Times*.

Electronic submissions only at www.appalachianheritage.net

Distributed by the University of North Carolina Press. Basic subscription price: $30/year for individuals, $40/year for institutions. For subscription requests and inquiries, visit the magazine's website, email uncpress_journals@unc.edu, or call 919.962.4201.

CONTENTS

CRAFT ESSAY

BOOK REVIEWS

COVER PHOTOGRAPH

Kopana Terry, *Hanging Wool*

EDITOR'S NOTE

JASON HOWARD

Ask any fiction writer and they will likely tell you there are glimpses of themselves in nearly every character they create. Their obsessions, desires, and fears are often tucked away in the shadows and clefts of their characters, a small part of the fictional whole. Readers are left to wonder and guess about which details and characteristics might be autobiographical or pure fiction, and according to most novelists, they are usually wrong.

But let's entertain this comparison between Denise Giardina and Carrie Bishop, one of the large cast of characters in Giardina's 1987 bestselling novel *Storming Heaven*. "I have traveled outside the mountains, but never lived apart from them," Bishop proclaims. "I always feared the mountains would be as jealous, as unforgiving, as any spurned lover. Leave them and they may never take you back. Besides, I never felt a need to go. There is enough to study in these hills to last a lifetime."

Unlike Bishop, Denise Giardina did leave Appalachia. As a searching twenty-something in the 1970s, she set off for Washington, D.C., enrolling in the Virginia Theological Seminary in Alexandria. After receiving her Masters in Divinity in 1979, she felt the call to write and began working as a secretary to fund her true vocation. Her time in Washington made her a writer, she has said, and in 1984 her first novel, *Good King Harry*, was published to positive reviews.

But like Bishop, Giardina seemed to realize the jealousy of the mountains. Homesick, she returned to West Virginia in the mid-eighties. More acclaimed novels, set both inside and outside Appalachia, have followed over the years—*Storming Heaven* (1987), *The Unquiet Earth* (1992), *Saints and Villains* (1998), *Fallam's Secret* (2003), and most recently, *Emily's Ghost* (2010)—cementing her reputation as one of the country's finest living authors.

But did the hills welcome her back? Or, perhaps more accurately, has she been content to be back? Those are complicated questions, Giardina would readily admit, as she has often found herself a stranger to her own culture as a political radical in what she views as an increasingly reactionary region and as one of the foremost critics of the coal industry when many are raging against a perceived "War on Coal." And yet she loves Appalachia to the bone.

Such complex themes are at the center of the special section devoted to her as this year's featured author. In "Candy," a chapter from her memoir-in-progress, she writes of her grandparents' struggle to finally leave their native Sicily and settle in West Virginia—a haunting parallel to her own struggle to find home. In her essay "A Mountaintop Experience," Giardina merges her theology and activism to create an unflinching spiritual critique of mountaintop removal mining. In "Mourning in the Mountains," a piece of commentary about the Upper Big Branch Mine disaster, she decries the lack of regulatory enforcement and attention paid to Appalachia from the media and federal government. And in our interview, she muses about her struggle to find hope for the region today.

Giardina's writing is complemented throughout the magazine by the powerful work of other writers. Robert Gipe, winner of the 2015 Weatherford Award in Fiction, contributes "Gone to Water," an excerpt from his novel-in-progress; acclaimed short fiction writer Elaine Fowler Palencia offers the haunting story "Dark Stars"; and O. Henry Prize winner Elizabeth Genovise writes about "The Fullback." With great candor, Darius Stewart chronicles confronting addiction in his essay "Seeing Pink Elephants." Ron Houchin, winner of the 2013 Weatherford Award in Poetry, contributes a series of mesmerizing poems, alongside sterling contributions from poets including Ida Stewart, Katherine Smith, and Br. Paul Quenon. Finally, Charles Green ponders the origin of literary ideas in his fascinating craft essay "Made Out of Words."

For Giardina, she has always found herself surrounded by ideas. To that end, she might agree with Carrie Bishop that there is indeed "enough to study in these hills to last a lifetime." ■

CANDY

DENISE GIARDINA

My mother and father suffered a contentious marriage. I now see Candy as an emblem of their fractures. Candy was an auburn cocker spaniel, my father's dog before he married my mother. To understand my dad, I have to understand his love for Candy.

My father was born in the United States, but returned to Sicily with his family when he was still an infant. My grandfather Sam was lured to West Virginia to work in the coal mines. He came from a poor village on the north coast of Sicily, San Giorgio near Patti, and he wanted out. The coal company would pay his passage and he would come to America, where he would certainly become rich.

Instead he dug coal, one of the most backbreaking and dangerous jobs possible, for little pay. He met Rosarin Peruzzi, called Sara, a young woman from another immigrant Sicilian family, in their McDowell County coal camp. She had memories of cooking for a well-to-do family in Palermo. Hard, now, to come by artichokes, pungent olives and decent olive oil, calamari, baccala. And vino. She, too, had come down in the world. Sam and Sara married and produced several children. My father was the youngest. Then they went back home.

■ ■ ■

According to Homer, Scylla was a monster that dwelt in the narrow strait between the Italian boot and Sicily, a monster who was also a cliff. Charybdis was also a monster, and a whirlpool, closer to Sicily. Any attempt by a ship to avoid one would lead to destruction by the other. Between Scylla and Charybdis was the Sicilian dilemma, what Appalachian culture would call between a rock and a hard place.

It is a myth that everyone who came to this country in search of a better life was happy with what they found. It is a myth that everyone thought, *This place, wonderful America, is far better than where I came from.* Sam and Sara did not think so. Somehow, and it must have cost them dearly, they were able to come up with the means to return to Sicily. They stayed ten years.

They named my father, born in West Virginia but raised in Sicily, Tindaro. I only learned why decades after his death. They had longed to return to Patti, a town that sprung up after an earlier, ancient settlement going back to the Greeks was abandoned because of the encroaching ocean. The ancient Greek town was Tyndaris. At some point a statue of Madonna and child arrived from Africa, and was lodged inside a church. The church, fortunately located on higher ground, survived the loss of Tyndaris to the sea, and still stands. It houses the statue, the ancient statue, of a black Madonna and child. Madonna Tindari, the name enduring. She was a saint; she was a Madonna, a conflation. She was perhaps originally from Ethiopia, she is black, and she holds her black Jesus proudly in front of her. A Latin inscription in gold fronts her: NIGRA SUM SED FORMOSA. I am black but beautiful. The "but" rather than "and" a sign of defensiveness, but pride nevertheless.

Pilgrims prayed to her statue. One local legend both calls out and rebukes racism: a pilgrim who arrived refused to pray to the Madonna after realizing she was black. As the pilgrim was leaving she accidentally dropped her baby into the encroaching ocean. Madonna Tindari caused the land to rise to form a lagoon and save the baby. People have since named their children after her. Tindari, for girls, Tindaro for boys. Thus my father's name. In America, the name was officially changed to Dennis, as all Tindaris and Tindaros lost their names to forced American translation, and for some reason Dennis was preferred for the Tindaros. Though my father's family continued to call him Tindaro when referring to him affectionately.

The name is ironic for me, because my young-woman clashes with my father were often based upon my perception of his racism. I know now my father's name was meant to hold his family close again to Sicily, to little Patti, and to Africans. But his family could not survive there.

So my grandparents left the brutal certainty of a Sicilian tenant farm to return to the brutal uncertainty of a West Virginia coal camp. I could never ask them about the decision because they spoke little English. And my father's experiences in a West Virginia coal camp, where the races were segregated, wiped away Tindaro and allowed Dennis to enter. Dennis, the Italian now in America, was often pitted against black boys in his coal camp, each facing discrimination and fighting for second place. Neither could have been to blame, but he carried some bad memories of fistfights that he never disclosed. No trace of his connection to Africa was passed on to his children in those days. Perhaps he had forgot it himself, or chose to forget.

■ ■ ■

Nona Sara always seemed difficult to me. It was not just because her English was poor. She was a force, and my *Nono* Sammie seemed almost a child beside her. Though my cousin told me that they had once had magnificent fights, but *Nono* Sammie had surrendered and chosen the path of least resistance. I wondered if the decision to return to West Virginia had been hers. Perhaps there were clashes with in-laws in Sicily. Perhaps she missed her relatives still here in the coal camps, or thought her children would have more opportunity here. Perhaps they were, in fact, starving in that poor Sicilian village. In any event, they left Sicily for good. The only memory of that time I could coax from my father, who always had difficulty expressing deep emotions in English, was he'd had to abandon a beloved donkey in Sicily, and that had broken his heart.

■ ■ ■

At age ten my father, who spoke no English, found himself in a first grade class in Welch, West Virginia. His teacher, Mrs. Sutcliffe, saw something in him. I met her years later when I was in high school, after she'd retired and moved to Charleston, where my family had also relocated. She said she'd called upon my dad as an enforcer. She was not a particularly good disciplinarian. But my father was twice as big as the other boys, so when the class got out of hand, Mrs. Sutcliffe would have him stand, fold his arms, and walk around the room glaring at the troublemakers. The class of six-year-olds would fall silent. Mrs. Sutcliffe spent extra time outside of class tutoring my father in English. He always spoke her name as though invoking a saint, and many years later he wept when she died, the only time I saw him cry.

We never knew my dad's exact birthdate—his family had not taken particular note when he arrived on the scene. So we celebrated his birthday on New Year's Day, and based on the memory of an older brother estimated the year to be 1911, eleven years before my mother. Though my father insisted he had been born in 1919. That was the year that he had actually arrived back in the United States. Perhaps he was trying to lessen the distance from my mother, which seemed far enough as it was, and to grow as the years passed. Perhaps he saw his return as a new birth.

My father came of age in rough times. Much of the country was booming after the war, spending freely and partying despite Prohibition, as oblivious to the coming Depression as a late-night carouser aboard the Titanic. But not so in West Virginia, which has never been in sync with whatever time in which it exists. After years of post-war turmoil, socialism was still popular in West Virginia, the miners' union was broken, wages continued low and safety conditions poor. Massive mine explosions claimed scores of lives. Italians faced discrimination, and taunts of "wop" and "dago".

For my father and his siblings, choices must be made. The two oldest boys, Giuseppe (Joe) and Francisco (Frank) were teenagers who spoke no English, and sending them to school seemed unpromising. Besides, their income was needed. So they went into the mines with Sammie. Joe worked for many years, but after years of facing the danger fled to Detroit to work in a factory, then on to Los Angeles, where he opened a red-sauce pasta restaurant in the San Fernando Valley. The oldest sister, Josie, escaped to Detroit as well. The next son,

He always spoke her name as though invoking a saint, and many years later he wept when she died, the only time I saw him cry.

Francisco (Frank) continued in the mines, because someone must help support the family, and he didn't know what else to do. Decades later, his black lungs clogged with coal dust, he would literally drown in his hospital bed.

For my father, both choices seemed impossible. Scylla and Charybdis again. He didn't want to leave West Virginia. But he knew the dangers of coal mining, and he was claustrophobic. When, during my childhood, we took a vacation that led us to a guided tour of an underground limestone cavern, he could not bring himself to go inside. He waited in the car, nervously smoking a cigarette, and was very quiet after we returned, as though relieved we had survived. Had he tried to enter a coal mine, he thought he might die of a heart attack.

Again his beloved first-grade teacher, Mrs. Sutcliffe, came to the rescue after his high school graduation. Her husband was a mining executive who arranged for my father to attend a two-year business program in Bowling Green, Kentucky, at what later became Western Kentucky University, paid for by the coal company if he would return to West Virginia and work for that company as an accountant. My father was good with numbers. He could control numbers. He did not have to use either Sicilian dialect or English to communicate with numbers. He is the only person I've ever known who enjoyed doing his income taxes each year. He gladly accepted.

■ ■ ■

As was his father before him, my father was a lady's man. I have seen pictures of him when he was young. He was athletic, and played on the high school basketball team. (When my brother and I were young, we did not believe our short, tubby father had played on a high school team, despite the photograph he showed us. My father had a basketball goal built in the backyard. When it was done, he walked around, dribbling a ball on the grass, sinking shot after shot. Then, we believed.) He was sloe-eyed, with a round face and curly black hair. My mother later claimed he had dated, and slept with, half the women in the county. She met him on a blind date, just before Pearl Harbor. She was from another world, rural eastern Kentucky, where there were very few Italians and those only in a handful of towns. My mother had never eaten pasta. Though they had one thing in common. He'd mourned his childhood donkey; she'd lost a beloved mule, sold during the Depression when her family was desperate for money.

Because of the Depression, my mother's family moved from their Kentucky farm to West Virginia, where my grandfather took a job managing a coal company store. My mother was in her early twenties, not long out of nursing school, and my father was already well into his thirties. She proudly claimed she refused his sexual overtures, and she seemed to think that had intrigued him enough to propose. (This reasoning did not impress me.) Then the war came and they separated. My father served on the European front, my mother as a nurse in the Philippines.

My mother occasionally reminisced about nursing POWs returned from the Japanese prison camps, and dating a variety of soldiers. I included some of her memories in my novel *The Unquiet Earth*. My father was posted to the Signal Corps in North Africa, and after the invasion of Sicily, he was used as an interpreter. Because the British Army was short on Italians, he was often loaned to General Montgomery, who later gave him a medal of thanks. A number of his fellow interpreters, mostly immigrants who had landed in large cities like New York and Chicago, became lifelong friends.

My father loved going back to Sicily during the war, so much so that though it was a war, and a terrible one, it seemed like a time he cherished. Indeed, it was an exciting time, a period of growth and exploration, for both my parents, the great adventure of their lives. That was what I gathered as a child. When I later came across accounts of the horrors of Iwo Jima, Bataan, Monte Cassino, Auschwitz, I was shocked. World War II had not been fun after all.

■ ■ ■

As soon as the war was over, my father acquired a dog, Candy the cocker spaniel. In the 1940s, cockers were the most popular dogs in America. My father had helped win a world war; their sheer numbers and their cultural contributions had finally accepted once-despised Italians. (Look now—Joe DiMaggio and Frank Sinatra and Dean Martin! Although my father would adamantly refuse to change his name from the

Italian as Dino "Martin", nee Crocetti, had done, shamefully to my father's mind. I often think of that, gratefully, even as I am forced for the ten-thousandth time to spell out my name for people. And even though a high school teacher once called me a "wop", I was proud of being half-Italian and proud that my father was proud.)

My father reclaimed a coal company job that would place him solidly in the middle class. He loved animals, and he deserved America's most popular dog. Candy came first, and then he married my mother. They moved to the coal camp of Black Wolf in McDowell County, West Virginia.

Perhaps after serving in the Philippines, she saw herself as worldly and adventurous, ready to engage with someone so very different from what she'd known.

I never really understood how they got back together. They bumped into each other by accident, but why did they bond again? Was it because the war was over and the available mates who had survived were being snapped up, right and left? What about all those soldiers my mother claimed she dated in the Philippines? Somehow, they hadn't panned out. She did admit to particularly pining for an Irishman named O'Sullivan from New Orleans. Apparently he pledged undying love, but when he returned home, she never heard from him again. So she accepted my father, the blind date she'd met before the war. My mother used to claim that the men in her family, and the neighbor boys she knew back in Kentucky, begged her not to marry "that Eye-talian." She claimed the young men of Feds Creek offered themselves as substitutes, to save her honor. I never quite believed that, for she obviously accepted none of them, if they were available. But I did believe that her family was not happy with her choice of husband. For several reasons, most, but not all of them based on ethnic prejudice.

And my father? She might have fascinated him because she was old family Appalachian, the place he identified with but did not quite belong to despite his love for hillbilly and gospel music. Her family was large and close, and I always sensed he admired them greatly, wanted to belong.

But my parents had very little in common that would have seemed to draw them together. Perhaps my mother was rebelling against all those men and boys back home who wanted to dictate and limit her future; stubbornness and rebelliousness were her most endearing and enduring qualities. Perhaps she sensed that my father, despite his shortcomings, had one great advantage—unlike many men, he would never try to run her life or hold her back. I never once saw my dad try to bully my mom, never try to block any of her plans or dreams.

Perhaps my mother's relationship with her own family was more problematic than she later let on. She tried to paint a picture to me of nostalgic times on the Homeplace in Pike County, Kentucky, which they lost to the Depression, though as I grew older I began to doubt it was all so rosy. Perhaps after serving in the Philippines, she saw herself as worldly and adventurous, ready to engage with someone so very different from what she'd known. Perhaps she just wanted to try pasta for the first time. Anyway, my mother married, not in a formal wedding gown, but in a prim white suit, with a reception of punch and cookies in the basement of a coal camp Methodist church. Certainly my father's family would have preferred a traditional Catholic ceremony, but such things were not important to my father in those days. So in 1946, flush with money from a new coal company job, he whisked my mother off to New York City (which he discovered during the war and fell in love with) for their honeymoon, neon lights and that first taste of pasta.

■ ■ ■

I arrived after five years, a bit late. My mother was desperate that I should arrive at once, and claimed she never once tried any sort of birth control. But nothing happened. She made fruitless trips to the doctor. One suggestion was that my father had a low sperm count. Finally she resigned herself to adoption. Suddenly, I appeared. I seemed to go a good ways toward mending the rift with her family.

My mother always made clear to me the wonder of my birth, after all those years of trying, those scarce sperm seeking in vain to penetrate her egg. Perhaps that warped my sense of myself, that I was somehow special in the scheme of things. Mom said that when the first television arrived in our house, while I was still an infant, I resented it. When my mother stared at the screen, I grabbed her chin and tried to direct her gaze to me.

■ ■ ■

Despite my father's position as bookkeeper, we lived in a coal camp house in Black Wolf with four rooms, just like those of the miners. Kitchen, two bedrooms, and living room, with a closet-sized add-on for the coal furnace that heated the radiators and a bathtub in the enclosure next to that. The only room for a wringer-washing machine was the front porch.

And there was Candy. By the time I entered grade school, Candy was old, fat and smelly. Her teats, which were hardened, especially disgusted me, peeling scabs that I disdained to touch.

Candy was cranky, and she ignored children. She didn't like to play or have adventures like the dogs on television, Rin-Tin-Tin and Lassie. I couldn't imagine Candy rescuing anyone like those dogs did. And as long as Candy lived, we could never have a real dog. My dad wouldn't allow the competition; he said it would upset Candy, who he adored.

My mother hated the Cocker Spaniel. Candy spread fleas, which got on all of us, because she lived in the house and there was no treatment for fleas that we knew of. I can recall my angry mother picking fleas off of us and crushing them between her fingernails before we settled into bed, and upending carpets to hoover up white clots of flea eggs. She had been raised on an eastern Kentucky farm. There, cats lived in the barn, to prey on vermin, and dogs stayed under the house or on the porch. Animals never came indoors with people. Candy's presence was a shock to her.

I believe mom might have been jealous as well. I never saw my father embrace my mother, never saw him kiss her. But Candy spent the evenings sprawled on the couch beside my dad while he read the paper or watched TV. He rubbed Candy's ears, scratched her scabby belly. Mom ignored them both and concentrated on me.

■ ■ ■

Still my mother also loved animals and was determined her children would have pets. She was partial to cats and other animals. With our orange tabby Tiger dead, failure there, my mom bought a parakeet at the local Murphy's five and dime. Petey had a cage where he spent his days, but at night, after the house was shut up tight, he was allowed out to fly about. He loved to fly to the bathroom and perch on the shower curtain rod while my mother bathed me and my brother, who had arrived three years later as unexpectedly as I had. I suspect, knowing now Petey was a bird meant for the tropics and not West Virginia winters in a drafty coal camp house, he enjoyed the steamy heat of the tiny bathroom.

But one evening he left the curtain rod for the floor, and we weren't paying attention. Candy was. After a search we found Petey beside the commode, bloody circles in his blue-feathered chest where Candy had bitten into him. From then on, I hated Candy as much as my mother did. ■

AN *APPALACHIAN HERITAGE* INTERVIEW

DENISE GIARDINA

Denise Giardina is not one to mince words. For nearly four decades, she has been speaking truth to power throughout Appalachia and beyond in her art and social activism, and for a short time, even on the political stump as the Mountain Party candidate for governor of West Virginia. A consummate student of literature, culture, history, and politics—subjects at the forefront of her six novels and many essays—she often underscores her opinions in person with a wry smile or a knowing look.

In this recent conversation with *Appalachian Heritage* editor Jason Howard, Giardina does not hold back, offering insight into her writing, how she defines the boundaries of Appalachian literature, her criticism of the coal industry, and what she believes the 2016 presidential election has revealed about the state of Appalachia and rural America.

■ ■ ■

JASON HOWARD: In your novel *The Unquiet Earth,* one of your characters, who is living in Washington, D.C., confesses, "I crave the mountains. They invade my dreams, and so do my kin, living and dead." Has this proven true for you as well?

DENISE GIARDINA: It has. It's why I'm back in West Virginia since 1992, despite my reservations. I still after all these years debate whether I did the right thing. But kin and the mountains called me back.

JH: You yourself left the mountains for a time earlier in your career, living, attending seminary, and working in and around Washington, D.C. How did that experience shape you as a writer and activist?

DG: I could not have become a writer if I hadn't gone to seminary and to Washington, D.C. The immersion in theology was essential to my writing. Washington threw me into politics and protest, and into joining a radical Christian fellowship, Sojourners. It got me arrested and sent to the D.C. jail. It faced me up against the powers and principalities. When it came time to write *Storming Heaven,* I was ready.

Denise Giardina

JH: Why were you arrested? Have you drawn on that experience throughout your subsequent years of activism?

DG: The Sheraton on—I think—Connecticut Avenue was hosting an arms show where [arms] dealers displayed their wares and countries came to buy. Kind of a demonic car show. We were protesting that. I had mixed feelings about the experience. I thought and still do [think] that we were right. We women were thrown in a paddy wagon along with some prostitutes (mostly drug addicts). At the jail holding cell we bonded and and started singing loud righteous activist hymns and civil rights songs. We were clapping and rocking and a guard showed up and told we'd be taken "out back" if we didn't shut up. As he left, one of the prostitutes yelled, "Well, it's only the Gospel." One of the seminal moments of my life. But I also realized after getting out the next day when our friends and lawyers posted bond that we had been playing jail, and the prostitutes were in jail for real.

JH: Why were you never able to stay gone? What brought you back to the mountains?

DG: This may be weird to say, but mountains feel like part of my physical body. I had to come back. Mountaintop removal is like ripping my guts out.

JH: As a writer from Appalachia, you have not felt constrained in your work by the region's borders. *Storming Heaven* and *The Unquiet Earth* are mostly set in the region. *Fallam's Secret* takes place in Stuart England and West Virginia. And *Good King Harry, Saints and Villains,* and *Emily's Ghost* are set outside the mountains. For a piece of writing to be labeled "Appalachian," do you think it must be set in the region?

DG: No. Growing up in the region affected every one of those novels. And *Storming Heaven* and *The Unquiet Earth* are not "Appalachian," they are about the world.

JH: Your most recent book, *Emily's Ghost,* was about Emily Bronte and how she often defied the social conventions of her day in terms of religion, courtship and marriage, and labor rights. I've heard you say that you see Emily Bronte as Appalachian, and that *Wuthering Heights* could even be considered an Appalachian novel. What do you mean by that?

DG: *Wuthering Heights* was ignored for decades because it didn't fit the English novel mode—too passionate, the servants too upfront and disrespectful, etc. I was intrigued to learn that George Washington was Emily's hero. I imagined her on the Appalachian frontier and thought she'd do just fine, and her novel would have fit just fine.

JH: You've written about the visual representation of Appalachians in media and the impacts they have had on you. What are some good, positive media representations of Appalachia on film or television?

DG: I like the first part of *Coal Miner's Daughter*. *Matewan* is good, although the small budget meant [director John] Sayles couldn't really capture the scope of what was happening. I thought *October Sky* was respectful, but totally ignored the political impact that is so important.

JH: I know you're a big Marshall football fan. How did you feel about the film *We Are Marshall*?

"A captivating novel that pulls at the heartstrings."

—Deseret News

DG: It didn't get good reviews but I thought it deserved better. The weakest part was some of the fictional characters. But this was before Matthew McConaughey had a career reversal, and his performance deserved attention it didn't get. Matthew Fox also gave a good performance. The movie captured the community, with respect, and also captured the times. (I was a college student in the early 1970s). When I watched the movie in a packed local theater, people wept.

JH: You've written a play before, but for the past couple of years you have been in front of the curtain, on stage in a program about Minnie Pearl for the West Virginia Humanities Council's *History Alive!* series. What is it about this comedienne that appeals to you?

DG: Well, we have same birthday. And we've both had breast cancer. But I just love her sweetness and humor. I'm a political person, but Minnie points us beyond politics to something that I think is higher—our common humanity. She touches a nostalgic part of America that we need to hold onto. Plus she was a pioneer in the field of female comics.

JH: Since the 1980s, you've written extensively in publications like *The Washington Post, The Nation, The New York Times,* and *The Charleston Gazette* about the environmental and economic exploitation of Appalachia. In 2000, you even ran for governor of West Virginia as the Mountain Party candidate to bring attention to what you have called "the horror of mountaintop removal." All these years later, do you think anything has changed in the region with regard to these issues?

DG: Sadly, no. We have destroyed our region and I fear it's too late.

JH: Do you see a connection between the social and political issues Appalachia is currently confronting with those that the nation as a whole is facing?

DG: I think Trump's candidacy shows there is a crisis in rural America nationwide. It's not new actually. Analyzing the past several elections, there are not really really red or blue states. Urban America, even in the Deep South, is blue. Rural America, even in the North, is red. And since Appalachian America is rural, it is red. Despite its own self interest.

JH: You said that Trump's candidacy has exposed "a crisis in rural America." What do you mean by that, and what should we and our political leaders be doing about it?

DG: To be honest I am discouraged. The experience of many rural Americans is so far removed from what urban Americans experience. Although the media reaches all corners [so] maybe the divide is more generational. But when you look at the election maps, rural areas always go right-wing. I think it would take something on the scale of the Marshall Plan to change that.

JH: In recent years you have grown more outspoken in your criticism of some aspects of contemporary Appalachian culture, and you've talked about how hard it is sometimes to live in Charleston. What makes you stay?

DG: I'm poor! Seriously, if I could afford it I don't know if I would leave or not. I'd certainly consider it. What I've seen is people who once fought against their situation now not only embracing it but attacking those who try to help. That's depressing.

JH: Journalists are constantly writing pieces on Appalachia and talking about the feelings of "hopelessness" in and about the region. What gives you hope for the region?

DG: It's bifurcated. I frankly have no hope for the coal mining areas. The non-coal areas have a lot of hope, a lot to offer. Someday they will figure out how to rehabilitate the coal mining areas. But it won't be for several generations or more. ■

A MOUNTAINTOP EXPERIENCE

DENISE GIARDINA

When God created heaven and earth, he looked at his handiwork and declared it "good." Each act of creation received this word of divine satisfaction. As time passed, only one part of God's creation became the subject of disappointment and anger—ourselves. But after the destruction of the Flood, God declared he would not repeat this act. As Christians, we believe that God even took human form in order to redeem us. The apostle Paul believed that redemption extended to the whole of creation. ("The creation itself will be set free from its bondage to decay..."—Romans 8:21).

Throughout time God has shown his continued love for creation. But God seems to have a special love for mountains. Time and again, when God wants to meet Man, he chooses mountains. Abraham was asked to sacrifice Isaac on a mountain. Moses was called to receive the Ten Commandments upon a mountain, and God showed him the Promised Land from a mountain. Jesus preached his greatest sermon upon a mountain. Monks in medieval England and Ireland saw mountains as "thin places," places where it is especially easy to pray and communicate with God. Psalm 68 even speaks of God having a mountain for his abode.

As a beloved part of creation, mountains themselves have been seen as participating in praising and thanking God. In the Psalms and elsewhere, the mountains and hills are described as skipping for joy. If we may speak to God from atop a mountain, the mountains themselves also sing praise to their Creator in their own special language.

Mountains have also given us enduring spiritual metaphors. Paul, in his first letter to the Corinthians, speaks of a faith that can move mountains (I Corinthians 13:2), though he goes on to add that without love, such faith is meaningless. Paul here is speaking of faith so strong it can accomplish the impossible. Moving mountains was meant to stay just that—impossible.

What then can we say about mountaintop removal? First we must acknowledge that man has indeed developed the capability to move mountains. We have that capability—but should we exercise it? Clearly God did not mean that we should, for to literally move a mountains makes the metaphor meaningless.

But mountaintop removal does far more spiritual damage than the destruction of language. The Appalachian Mountains, according to geologists, are among the oldest in the world. This means they are among the first mountains God created. The beautiful Appalachians are a balm to the soul. Their destruction speaks of the soul's sickness.

If God loves mountains so much, and Scripture is clear that he does, how must we grieve him when we destroy them? When Scripture bids us look up to the hills, from whence comes our help, how may we when those hills are gone? Where is hope or comfort then, when the signs of hope given by God, the mountains, have been leveled?

Psalm 24 tell us that the earth, and the fullness thereof, belongs to the Lord. Woe on us if we continue to destroy what is the Lord's. But the woe, the shame, is for more than just disobeying God. When we destroy the beautiful, the sacred mountains, we reject God's gift. It is a gift near to the heart of God. To destroy the mountains is to spit in the face of God. It must break his heart. ■

MOURNING
IN THE MOUNTAINS

DENISE GIARDINA

(2010)

People in West Virginia had hoped that on Monday night we would gather around televisions with family and friends to watch our beloved Mountaineers face Butler in our first chance at the men's N.C.A.A. basketball title since 1959. Men working evening shifts in the coal mines would get to listen thanks to radio coverage piped in from the surface. Expectations ran high; even

President Obama, surveying the Final Four, predicted West Virginia would win.

Then, on Tuesday morning, we would wake to triumphant headlines in sports pages across the country. At last, we would say, something good has happened to West Virginia. The whole nation would see us in a new light. And we would cry.

Instead, halfway through Saturday night's semifinal against Duke, our star forward, Da'Sean Butler, tore a ligament in his knee, and the Mountaineers crumbled. And on Monday evening, while Duke and Butler played in what for us was now merely a game, West Virginians gathered around televisions to watch news of a coal mine disaster.

On Tuesday, the headline in *The Charleston Gazette* read instead: Miners Dead, Missing in Raleigh Explosion. And we cried.

Despite the sunny skies and unseasonably warm weather, the mood here in southern West Virginia is subdued. As of Tuesday afternoon, twenty-five men have been confirmed dead, two are critically injured, and four are missing and presumed dead. Their fellow West Virginians work round the clock and risk their own lives to retrieve the bodies.

Already outrage is focused on Massey Energy, owner of the Upper Big Branch mine. Massey has a history of negligence, and Upper Big Branch has often been cited in recent years for problems, including failure to properly vent methane gas, which officials say might have been the cause of Monday's explosion.

It seems we can't escape our heritage. I grew up in a coal camp in the southern part of the state. Every day my school bus drove past a sign posted by the local coal company keeping tally, like a basketball scoreboard, of "man hours" lost to accidents. From time to time classmates whose fathers had been killed or maimed would disappear, their families gone elsewhere to seek work.

We knew then, and know now, that we are a national sacrifice area. We mine coal despite the danger to miners, the damage to the environment and the monomaniacal control of an industry that keeps economic diversity from flourishing here. We do it because America says it needs the coal we provide.

West Virginians get little thanks in return. Our miners have historically received little protection, and our politicians remain subservient to Big Coal. Meanwhile, West Virginia is either ignored by the rest of the nation or is the butt of jokes about ignorant hillbillies.

Here in West Virginia we will forget our fleeting dream of basketball glory and get about the business of mourning. It is, after all, something we do very well. In the area around the Upper Big Branch, families of the dead will gather in churches and their neighbors will come to pray with them. They will go home, and the same neighbors will show up bearing platters of fried chicken and potato salad and cakes. The funeral homes will be jammed, the mourners in their best suits and ties and Sunday dresses.

And perhaps this time President Obama and Americans will pay attention, and notice West Virginia at last. ■

SURFACE MINE

Some trees in extremity.
Some branches like a woman's arm bared

on the tattoo table,
her skin an ink sink

gone here to kin, here
to spirits, here to dread.

Some trees shed
like it's nothing,

bestowing by the trunkful
even as the weather's coming

scarves of bark
that look like the wind might

were it dried and
cured of itself.

IDA STEWART

RADISH

Halve it: white
meat, prickling heat:
bead of sweat
of a fingernail
down the back
of my neck
and the path
I've knived through
the weedy division
between two radi-
o stations that is
spring, that is
what spring forces
from its pores,
our pores: vapor,
salt, and the
country, come to
grips, finds its
spine, snaps back
sudden as a
limb across a
child's chest—*shh*—
the way what's
pronounced shelters what's
silent in *fight*.

IDA STEWART

FROM "THE TIDE POOLS"

Open sesame:
open season on thick skin:
a narrow hand as

good as snow melting
on the scruff: the neck as good
as the high field where

the men wait, having
divided from themselves all
traces of themselves

down to the antler-
velvet frost that dawn now burns
from around their boots.

IDA STEWART

GONE TO WATER

ROBERT GIPE

God didn't give us no lakes in Canard County. Too much downhill, too much push to the water. So when the government decided we could use some help, they dammed up our rivers and they made us lakes. Had us make them. The people I come from were good enough to push the dirt around, to make piles where a man in a white shirt and a government sedan said *make piles.*

But what do I know about all that? What I know is like scratches on rocks, shards of tales. I barely know who I come from. But I know this: the lakes in Tennessee are bigger. Way bigger. Big shots have houses around them. I know our lakes barely got enough to put a picnic shelter around. A ragged boat dock with a shack at its end where men spit in the same sawed-off two-liter bottle, listen to Bill Monroe, and talk about bodies found on the bottom of the lake and bodies never found. The company owned around our lakes, cause they still might be something worth taking from the mountains thereabouts. I'm sure there is. Orange water feeds our lakes. They are poor affairs.

I know this too: Hubert went to water when he was worried. He put on short pants and he went to water. Hubert had never given up on my mother. He remembered her the way I did, the way she was before my father died. I seen more love in Hubert over the years. He still kept to himself in that building his father built to hang out with his rusty gang of thieves and petty officials. All them gone now, and now Hubert had only me and sometimes Evie and Albert.

When the law took Sidney Coates's money and everybody said my mother informed on him, we figured Hubert would plan a picnic, have us all go to the lake. Cause it was picnic season, plus that is what Hubert did.

"I could use a picnic," Evie said. "Things is too tight around here."

Hubert grumbled something none of us caught, ended on the words "ice cream." So we figured a picnic was what was fixing to happen. But it wasn't.

We were sitting in that building Thursday afternoon, all of us on stumpy chunks of oak save Albert who sat on the back seat of an LTD. It was about two in the afternoon on the day after Belinda come to Momma's hollering at June about how she was gonna kill Momma.

Evie and Albert argued as usual, about something stupid like whether fish or birds was smarter. Hubert stood up said, "Let's go," and headed towards the barn door. We give him a head start. Hubert opened the passenger door of the Continental told Albert to drive. Me and Evie got in back and Hubert told Albert to head out towards the lake, but when we got to the picnic place, the shelters by the hauled-in beach, Hubert told Albert to keep going. Albert did, on up into what Evie called *Yesterdayland,* where folks kept bees, everybody played music, and nobody counted on the law to settle things.

Hubert's daddy was Green Jewell, and Green's mother was from up that way. Her people still had a place, still had land up there. But it was way far away from the Trail so hadn't none of us been out there much, so we was leaning on Hubert to tell us where to go, show us how to be.

Hubert said, "Turn in here."

We crossed a wood bridge. An old woman walked towards us with a dead snake hung over the blade of her hoe. Albert stopped the vehicle and she stood at Hubert's window.

Hubert said, "That's a nice one."

The woman said, "Never cared for snakes."

Hubert said, "How you doing, Peck?"

The woman said, "Hubert, I been worse."

Hubert said, "How's your garden?"

"Pitiful." Peck leaned down and looked at us. Stood back up, said "Who you got?"

Hubert pointed at me and Albert. "Him and her is Delbert's." He jerked his thumb at Evie. "She's a Bright."

Peck leaned down again, looked at Evie, said "My daddy courted a Bright. She run off with a gravel man in here building the dam."

Albert said, "Your daddy's better off."

Evie popped Albert on back of the head.

Hubert said, "We're going up to the falls, Peck. Why don't you come with us?"

Peck looked out over the place like an Indian in one of those paintings by a white man, one of them ones where the Indian looks all noble peering out over a canyon full of buffalo, noble even though he's in the middle of getting assfucked by a bunch of cowboys.

"Can't," she said. "Waiting on Shasta to bring me them babies. Untelling when she'll get here."

Hubert said, "Good to see you, Peck."

Peck said, "Good to see you too, Hubert." She probably would have said tell so-and-so hello, but Hubert didn't have nobody around him anymore and so Peck just stood there.

We grew up on tales of him shooting gun thugs from the woods above the road to mines on strike, tales of him tying scabs to the railroad track.

We drove past the place where I reckon Peck stayed given they was a garden on the side big as a grocery store parking lot with string-run beans and corn thigh-high and tomatoes already ganging on the vine. Then we went by a long house with white siding and storm windows and a two-vehicle carport. It was a nice house, a good liver's house, built solid, but it didn't look like nobody lived in it, nor had in a while—shingles blown off the roof, downspout come loose, sheets against the front windows.

Evie said, "Whose is that?"

Hubert said, "That's where my papaw lived."

Albert said, "Snatch?"

Hubert said, "What they called him."

Me and Albert had heard about Snatch, our father's grandfather. He was a union man. We grew up on tales of him shooting gun thugs from the woods above the road to mines on strike, tales of him tying scabs to the railroad track. The scabs' screams when the train cut them to pieces woke me many a night, even though the killings was long before I was born, back in the thirties. Hubert and Daddy had showed us the road where the company drug Snatch by a chain behind a truck to the state line, threw him over a hill into a den of snakes, left him for dead.

I remember Snatch in a hospital bed in the front room of Green's house, hooked up to oxygen cause of black lung, face grey as pipe. I come in crying one time when I was five. Albert'd run over one of my frogs on his Big Wheel and there was nobody home to cry to, only Snatch. Snatch opened his dinosaur eyes, raised up on his bed, tubes in his nose, stuck the broke-off stump of his right first finger at me said, "You better dry it up, Little Missy," said it to me like I was grown. It stayed with me from that day on. I was grown. Got that from Snatch.

"They called him Snatch cause it was what he loved the best," Albert grinned, his teeth like hominy. "Aint that right, Hubert?"

"Pull off here," Hubert said, pointing at a wide spot off the road. We was back in the woods by then, Highhead Mountain rising up above us like a preacher had the goods on us and fixing to lay us low. The pull-off spot was robed around with laurel and when we got out we had to duck and dodge through it.

Hubert got a red canvas bag out of the trunk of the Continental. Bag had a strap where you could sling it over your shoulder. Hubert headed up through a gap in the laurel, which closed up behind him. Albert scrambled after Hubert, fell, and then he was gone through the laurel.

Evie said, "What's he doing?"

I said nothing to Evie who once had been dear to me, now just part of my problem, part of everybody's problem. I didn't have a friend now and that was Evie's fault. Fault of them pills.

It was near-dark in the laurel. I could barely see the horned ghost of Albert's white wifebeater floating up the path, but I saw enough to follow, grabbing hold of roots and tree trunks, rocks and mud, til the path leveled off, skirted the hillside, and hooked right beside a creek running flat, past overhangs and rock towers, hiding places and lookouts enough for a hundred Indians and outlaws.

Hubert got going good once he got out in the woods, and I never did catch him and Albert, but little goat Evie caught me. She had trouble keeping pace, so she didn't say much, and we moved huffing and puffing through that church of woods til we got to where the trail swung up in our faces and we could hear the sound of the falls.

When we caught up to Hubert and Albert, Hubert's shorts dropped from his waist and naked Hubert stepped down into a pool eddying off the creek thirty feet below where the water crashed from a rock ledge seventy feet above. The waterfall landed in a rainbow spray and made the ferns and bushes and tree limbs in its sway shiver. Hubert's mouth made a little "o" as he slipped into the chill water up to his chest. Albert crouched above him on the trunk of a fallen tree, a monkey henchman floating in the summer sparkle.

Evie said, "What are you doing?"

Hubert's eyes were closed. He said, "I need y'all to pass through the water."

Evie said, "Do what?"

Hubert lay his arms out flat on the surface of the pool. "I need you to go through the falls and bring me back something."

Albert said, "All of us?"

Evie said, "Why we gonna do that?"

Hubert's eyes opened. He lay back in the pool, wetting the back of his head. "It's money," he said. Hubert floated and turned. "Lots and lots of money."

Albert come off his perch and rockscrambled towards the fall. Evie caught him before he reached the spray.

Hubert said, "You go too, Dawn," his eyes closed again. "Don't leave it to them two."

At the top of the waterfall, drops of water jumped free of the rest of the fall, but by the time the drops hit the rocks below, they were all in the same place. I followed Evie and Albert behind the sheet of water.

■ ■ ■

The money we found in the darkness behind the falls was duct taped inside two garbage bags. We followed Hubert down the creek to a wide place where the water flowed slow and the creek bed looked smooth shiny and hard as the floor in the courthouse lobby. We took the money out of the garbage bags. It had mold on it. Some of it you couldn't tell what it was.

Evie said, "This money is nasty."

Albert said, "I think something shit on it."

"Money's money," Hubert said. "It don't go bad."

We'd all asked Hubert over and over where it come from, and every time he acted like he hadn't heard us. I stopped asking him.

Evie said, "Do we have to wash every bill?"

Hubert said, "You don't have to wash none of it."

Evie said, "Shoo."

Hubert nodded.

Evie and Albert settled into cussing and picking at each other. They dipped the bills into the creek, their hands flat under the water, rubbing the presidents' faces back to life. Hubert moved from one tree to another, his hand against the trunks, bad leg dragging, grimacing.

Hubert leaned into my ear, grumbled, "So much racket."

I said, "That creek is so clean."

Hubert looked at the creek. His throat rattled like a stick drug across a metal grate. "Your mother," he said, walking away from the creek into the boulders, talking where I couldn't hear him.

Evie said to Albert, "You splash me one more time and I drown you. I ain't even kidding."

I said to Hubert library low, "Do what?" and followed him into the boulders, followed him back where it could be just me and him. I came around one boulder and he was sitting on another, his hands in moss, breathing hard.

I said, "You're hurting, aren't you?"

He drew his lips tight, said, "I don't know your mother's worth the investment."

I sat down beside him. I wanted to lean on him. I didn't.

Hubert looked at the creek. His throat rattled like a stick drug across a metal grate.

I said, "Does old money stay good?"

"It does," Hubert said. "Legal tender."

The tops of the trees rustled. The light sprinkled down like sugar.

"If Momma wasn't in trouble," I said, "what would you do with that money?"

Hubert sniffed. He wasn't crying, but his eyes were watery. "Nothing," he said. "It aint out here for using."

I didn't ask no more.

I said, "You don't smell like you're taking care of yourself."

Hubert coughed but nothing come up.

I said, "You getting enough to drink?"

Hubert said, "I reckon."

I said, "Smells like it."

Hubert looked at me sideways, said, "Why don't you go help your brother?"

I said, "Who else knows about this?"

Hubert didn't look up, said "I don't know. Too many lost years. Too many nights."

I leaned forward, my elbows on my knees. I stayed talking low, said, "What are you talking about?"

Hubert said, "Too many years in the wilderness."

"Hubert," I said. "You need to think about getting married."

Hubert turned his head to me, said, "You proposing?"

I said, "You're going to seed. You don't make no sense."

"I don't know who all I told," Hubert said. "They was years when I didn't care who knew what." Hubert stood up.

"Well," I said, "you couldn't of told too many. It's still here."

Hubert turned in his spot like a dog with arthritis winding up to sit down. "Don't care who knows," he said.

I wished Hubert would sit back down, but he went back and watched Evie and Albert wash money and before long Hubert told them to forget it, and we stuffed the money in the red canvas bag, and we trooped back down the creek.

When we got back to Hubert's place, June's little red Honda car was there.

When June seen Evie she said, "Missed you in class this week."

Evie said, "I know what we're supposed to do. I found out. We're supposed to write a paper. And I got me a topic now."

Hubert said, "I want you to take this back with you, June."

June looked at the red bag. We all did.

Story Hubert told was this: Cinderella had called Hubert said Sidney Coates hired a man in Stickerbush to make my mother disappear. Hubert called Sidney said what if Hubert put back the money Sidney had lost. Sidney said it'd be a start. People was scared of Hubert, but it don't pay to have that much money in the house, not when you had a June who could take it and make it safe.

"All right," she said.

We followed June in the Continental to the Virginia line. When June's car slipped down the hill, Albert pulled in behind a coal truck idling at the top of the hill. Hubert got out of the Continental and smoked a cigarette. And then we went back to the Trail. ■

GOSPEL RIVER

Despite my animosity toward Sunday
school and church: the huge helmets of grey hair
capped by tight buns, flung back in hallelujahs;
the spirit-filled oxblood wingtips loping
to and from hard seats, and all the cloth—
giant flowery dresses billowing up aisles,
flapping dark suits and long ties lolling
like colorful tongues, huge smothering drapes
on everything—I loved to sink into rows
of pews with others. Our round backs ached
and stretched against unforgiving waterlines
of wood as we flowed down the river of sorrow
and loss, yowling and drowning like wolves.

RON HOUCHIN

PISSING INITIALS ON SNOW

(Winter Solstice, Thursday, 22 December 1977)

Thinking about nothing but the weather,
I couldn't sleep or write. The last or the worst
was coming. I'd let pencil fall onto blank page

and taken the four-wheeler to rumble over
the clock-face of snow. I switched off the key
to hear flakes tick into the tree line, counting

toward better days. A two-foot depth lay
sighing under pines. Back, down the hollow
everyone rode a bed like a boat toward

the dim island where we spend a third
of our time. Clouds, picturesque and painful,
scrubbed around the moon. Not even God

in his long coat walked here, but I looked all
about anyway before unzipping thick coveralls.

RON HOUCHIN

TALKING TO SHADOWS

"...they will wield power in the smallest ways"
—Colm Toibin

Early evening, the first lamps light in dew
on grass. Before I've walked half the hill,
they're there among the streetlight's ellipsis,
the brocade of trees trying to remember
green, and the silence that avoids saying
anything that might reach ears.

To speak to shadows is to remain still
in their reshaping of the world. Long
limbs lengthen, slanting toward each other,
as if a hard wind pushes them over Earth.
A church tower crosses the road, only
its chimes reaching the last of daylight.

RON HOUCHIN

THE MATTER OF WORDS

Not just the spittle droplets and the vapor of breath
or the pauses wherein the questions grow,
but the weight freighted in the listening mind,
the change in brainwave patterns that turns
the thought into crankcase, the discussion
into filled warehouse pallets after lights and water
glasses have gone home, and all have taken off shoes,
had their nightcaps of Tanqueray and lime, begun
to forget in dream the first words, the thoughts
born, and the waning moon its hold on white.

RON HOUCHIN

DARK STARS

ELAINE FOWLER PALENCIA

"You see a lot of it in law enforcement," said Earl McClure, pouring himself another shot of Bulleit. "A family that one bad thing happens to, seemingly random, and then another and another, until it becomes a whole cluster of tragedies. And you don't know why. Why them."

Jimbo Hunter nodded. "Like dominoes falling."

They were sitting on Jimbo's deck in Poplar Hills subdivision outside Blue Valley, Kentucky, under a full moon and a brilliant salting of stars. It was a warm August night. From inside Jimbo's comfortable brick ranch house came the noise of whatever sitcom his wife Mary Jean was watching while she did her cross-stitch. Oblivious, Jimbo would later think, to what was coming. Him, too. When people imagine disasters, he'd realize, it's always from the point of view of a survivor.

Earl had walked through three back yards from his own house for the Bulleit Jimbo had won in a Men's Club cornhole tournament. Jimbo hated cornhole, which was basically a kid's game, why pretend it was anything else. Push come to shove, he didn't actually enjoy having a good time; but because of his position in the community, sometimes he couldn't avoid it.

He and Earl had been talking about the McFann family. Six of the eight children had straggled through Moore County High, of which Hunter had been principal until his retirement that spring. Now three of the McFanns were dead of several kinds of stupidity, or bad choices, as they were now called. Two more were in prison and the youngest boy, Ikey, the one who had potential, had been killed by a roadside bomb in Afghanistan. Jimbo had just quoted his mother on Mrs. McFann, who "went to sin slick as a ribbon" after her husband died of an aneurysm.

Earl hitched himself up in his lawn chair, causing Mr. Bojangles, the Lincairn terrier asleep at his feet, to shift and sigh. "Some families, it's like they're traveling under a dark star."

"And," Jimbo put in, "economics don't always come into it. Some kid whose family don't have jack will turn out fine, whereas in a family with money, them kids can grow up wilder than billy goats." He liked to mix in bad grammar when he talked to Earl, a relief after all the years of watching himself at school.

"Yet things do happen for a reason," Earl opined. "What goes under the Devil's belly comes up over the Devil's back."

"More'n likely," said Jimbo, though he knew it was lazy thinking.

Now, due to the pile-up of received wisdom, both men had the decency to be embarrassed and they fell silent. He can't think and drink, each concluded concerning the other man. Mr. Bojangles yawned, stretched, and wandered down to the bottom of the yard.

But the pull of story was too strong for the men to stay silent. Both felt it, like a belt across the chest that could only be loosened through swapping tales. It was the way people in the hills had always negotiated life: the oral tradition, scholars called it. Besides, each felt he was close, very close, to saying something profound.

Earl said, "One of Dad's first cases after we moved here was Ross Boatman. Same kind of a deal." Earl had followed his father into police work. When Jimbo didn't say anything, he added, "Boatman taught business at the college. Lived over on Second." He lit a cigarette, which he felt he could do with impunity since they had cut the bad part out of his lungs.

In the shadows, where Mr. Bojangles could be heard snuffling, stood the crabapple trees Jimbo had planted along Clay Creek, which bisected the neighborhood. Beyond the subdivision lay five miles of forest and then Poplar Flats, where nuclear waste had been buried in the late sixties, and farther on, just at the lower edge of night, the rounded hills particular to the Knobs region.

Finally Jimbo said, "I had Mrs. Boatman for fourth grade. It happened that year."

"I knew his first wife and daughter," said Earl. "After the divorce, they lived in those apartments up on Lewis Branch.

Both of them died in the Nada Tunnel, head-on collision with a farm truck. Like I said, some families are cursed."

But Jimbo wasn't listening. He had gone back to that week again. He had thought about it so many times that it had become a story he saw from all perspectives, as if he were the Watchmaker God he would believe in if He would only look up from His workbench and His fashioning of other universes and give a rat's ass for what was going on in this one.

In fourth grade, Jimbo figured out that if he did poorly, less would be expected of him. That gave him more time to play baseball and work on his models. His father whipped him when he started bringing bad grades home, but he didn't care. He liked outsmarting everybody by being dumb. Why he had set the Truesdells' garage on fire he didn't know to this day, though he recalled how prettily the flames leaped from the pile of gasoline-soaked rags he'd assembled. The sight had filled some empty place in him.

He couldn't let the grownups have the satisfaction of knowing how easily they had changed him back to his old good self.

His parents had been around the bend about it all and there was talk of sending him to live in Letcher County with Papaw and Mamaw Craft. But his teacher, the second Mrs. Boatman, who had married Mr. Boatman in her forties and had no children, came up with a different idea; and she lived only two blocks away.

Every weekday morning the summer after fourth grade, she required him to come to her house and sit on her side porch for one hour, reading some biography for children. She probably couldn't do it nowadays without a court order, Jimbo reflected, but the authority of teachers wasn't questioned then.

Each day when Mrs. Boatman came to tell him his reading time was up, he was to follow her into the kitchen, summarize for her what he'd read, and be served a snack of four vanilla wafers, and milk in a jelly glass with a faded picture of Bugs Bunny on the side.

It didn't take him long to be affected by the stories of men and women who had made something of themselves, though he stayed sullen and pretended he was still a bad boy. He couldn't let the grownups have the satisfaction of knowing how easily they had changed him back into his old good self.

That day he arrived on the porch with a kids' biography of Abraham Lincoln and got going without telling Mrs. Boatman he was there. As he lounged in the porch swing, keeping the motion going with an occasional foot push, he could hear water running in her kitchen, a radio playing classical music, and the low voices of Mr. and Mrs. Boatman talking together. Occasionally Mr. Boatman laughed in his pinched way, like a cat coughing. He had taught Jimbo to dunk the vanilla wafers in the milk.

Bees moved in the peach-colored roses outside the white picket porch railing. Down the street, someone was mowing a lawn. Sunlight crept across the wooden floor towards the swing. At the community pool, morning swim was starting. The Lincoln family, Jimbo read, moved from Kentucky to Indiana to get away from slavery. At Pigeon Creek they were poor and cooked their food over an open fire. Probably they didn't have an accelerant like gasoline. Jimbo had learned the word *accelerant* shortly after being caught by Mr. Truesdell as he watched the fire he'd set, with his father's lighter in his hand.

Of a sudden he decides he's had enough reading. The sun is too bright. The chigger bites on his legs itch. Surely an hour has gone by.

He opens the screen door and moves silently through the Boatmans' living room, a knock-kneed kid with an overbite and a buzz cut, wearing a Detroit Tigers tee shirt and khaki shorts. Then he's in Mrs. Boatman's point of view.

She's standing at the kitchen sink rinsing Mr. Boatman's hair. Her husband has a towel pinned around his shoulders like a cape and is leaning back in a swivel chair like ladies do in beauty parlors so that he's looking at the ceiling and his head is tilted back over the sink. The excess of the dye she's just colored his hair with is swirling down the drain like liquid coal dust.

When Mrs. Boatman sees Jimbo, she thinks in terror, *Why, it can't be!* Mr. Boatman was adamant about having his hair done this morning. She'd told him Jimbo Hunter was due for his reading lesson, causing him to snap, "Why do you want to fool with that little idjit?" but agree to wait till evening. Twenty minutes later, when no knock had come at the door, they mutually decided that the boy was playing hooky and it was safe to proceed. Given Jimbo's behavior that school year, she'd been expecting him to slack off.

But forget the mutual decision. She will be blamed for this. There will be consequences. No one, but no one, is allowed to know that Mr. Boatman dyes his hair. As she is thinking all this, Mr. Boatman sits up, sees Jimbo, and shrieks. Mrs. Boatman steps in front of her husband, blocking Jimbo's view, and says, "Run along home, Sugar. I'm got to be somewhere right now. We'll talk about your book on Monday."

Down by the creek, Mr. Bojangles was growling. Earl hoisted himself upright and said, "I'm 'on see what that fool dog's doing."

Jimbo's mind jumped to the next Saturday of that long-ago summer.

He's sitting on the front steps of his house, oiling his baseball glove. The week before, when he got home from the

Boatmans,' he'd told his mother why he had come home early and she had a good laugh. That was all he'd done. Surely it didn't matter. It's true that his mother was chuckling about Mr. Boatman's dye job with Mrs. Cassity the next day, but they weren't being mean. Now Mr. Boatman has disappeared.

In Jimbo's memory, the sun has set behind the hills above the college, leaving the northern sky clear and bright, like the backdrop for a play. It is the hour before Sunday supper. Caroline Avenue is quiet and empty but for the swish of a sprinkler rotating on the Denders' lawn. Someone is frying pork chops, the smell spreading over the neighborhood like a benediction. In the silence the modest houses body forth in their essential geometry, pillowed by yard trees that long ago walked in from the surrounding forest and took up residence. Then Jimbo sees a figure at the end of the block. At the sight of what the man is carrying, his skin shivers.

Coming to the head of the avenue, where it intersects Crescent Boulevard, Bruiser Jones slows his walk. He is reluctant to perform the task that awaits him. His bulldog face is shadowed by the brim of his sweat-stained fedora and the usual unlit stogie drags down one side of his mouth.

A tireless roamer, Bruiser is out and about at all hours. More than anyone, he knows what goes on in town and immediately beyond. If a car wreck happens out in the county at two a.m., Bruiser will more than likely be standing at the crash site, hands thrust in his pockets, rocking back and forth on his heels, when the police get there. Wits say he sees twice as much as anyone else because of his lazy right eye that is always looking elsewhere.

As Bruiser comes down the avenue in his gliding, cat-soft stride, surprising in such a big man, carrying two fishing rods, a tan raincoat and Mr. Boatman's creel, Miss Olive Humphrey steps out on her front porch and stands quietly, as if watching a funeral cortège pass. On the other side of the street from Jimbo, Dr. Don Rose comes around the side of his house with a pair of hedge clippers, does a double-take, and says something to Bruiser.

At that moment, Bruiser turns his head and Jimbo feels an invisible arrow from the wandering eye pass through him like lightning. Behind him, the screen door opens and his father walks past. He and Dr. Rose join Bruiser and the three men walk on.

His father doesn't return until after eight p.m. Jimbo is in the den, watching television. He turns the sound down so he can hear his parents talking in the kitchen.

"I've kept supper. Do you want milk or iced tea?" his mother asks.

"Tea," says his father. His chair scrapes. "He was in twelve feet of water, to the left of the spillway where the rocks go down. Bruiser said you could see him plain as day; the water was that clear. He'd folded his raincoat and laid his watch on top of it, next to his fishing tackle."

"His raincoat," says Jimbo's mother. The silverware drawer rattles.

"He must have gone up to the dam early, way before dawn. The coat was damp from the rain."

The oven door opens and shuts. "Did he slip?"

"Bruiser said he had horseshoes in his pockets. Not enough of 'em to weigh him down, but enough to show it was deliberate."

"What did Myra say?"

Myra was Mrs. Boatman.

"Oh, she turned on the waterworks, all right."

"She didn't have any idea?"

"No, the only thing she could think was, evidently he was upset over people finding out he dyed his hair. It was all over town this week. Is there any more meatloaf?"

"That's not news. Why, everybody knows it isn't his natural color," said Jimbo's mother. "You don't kill yourself over something like that."

Jimbo runs upstairs and belly-slides under his bed. Lying among the dust bunnies, he cries silently into the crook of his arm.

Now Earl came back to the deck and picked up his glass. "He's after a chipmunk or something," he reported of Mr. Bojangles.

"You ever hear a reason why Boatman drowned himself?" asked Jimbo.

"My opinion, he was always a little off."

They both knew what happened to Mrs. Boatman, so there was no need to tell it. She took a week off from school after Mr. Boatman's funeral, then returned to the fourth grade,

Earl said, "The concept of original sin in a pretty crude tool for explaining how things turn out."

never to speak of her husband's suicide. Jimbo had gone on to the fifth grade that fall. Maybe ten years later, when she went into early onset dementia, a niece moved her to Lexington, stuck her in the back bedroom of some defrocked nurse's house, stole the money the Boatmans willed to the college, and sold the antiques the couple had refinished together, along with the eight sterling silver mint julep cups that had been in Mrs. Boatman's family for a hundred years. With the Boatmans' money the niece built a big house near Midway with solid walnut floors.

Earl said, "The concept of original sin is a pretty crude tool for explaining how things turn out."

Whoa, thought Jimbo. He didn't want to get into religion. Earl read a lot over there by his lonesome. He was smarter than he looked, and you didn't want to match actual knowledge with him.

"Hey, I'd better get along. Thanks for the booze," said Earl, and slapped his leg to bring Mr. Bojangles to heel.

"Don't walk under any of them dark stars," joked Jimbo.

"Hell, they're the ones you don't see," said Earl.

He was halfway gone when he turned back to say, "There were stories about pictures."

"Pictures?"

"That Russ Boatman had. Of children."

So now Jimbo had to rethink his whole life, especially the career in education he undertook out of guilt over what he'd done to the Boatmans. And didn't this fact also disprove Earl's theory of undeserved tragedy? All at once he was sick of himself, his house, the night, everything.

Earl walked home by the street; it was too dark to go through back yards. Most of the neighbors were at least his age, and armed. They might not recognize him in moonlight through their bifocals. Blearily he ruminated on Jimbo, how he'd seemed preoccupied tonight. Maybe it was just the miserable fact of retirement. Or maybe there was more to tell. They had been on the edge of becoming confidential. Somebody said Jimbo had an eye on the oldest McFann girl when she was in high school. Earl was glad he hadn't spilled his own story of youthful stupidity, which he'd come so close to doing that he'd had to get up and pretend to check on Mr. Bojangles down by the creek. It was talking about the doomed McFanns that made him think of it, the way those boys used to tarzan around in a big sycamore in their front yard.

Earl sees himself up in the maple tree again, a thirty-year-old man with a gun waiting for Dr. Daniels to come home. The twins are eleven months old and Brenda has concluded for sure that they're both deaf. She and Earl have gone over her pregnancy and the births a hundred times, and each time it all looks fishier, like the way when Brenda started cramping at seven months Daniels told her to drink a double shot of vodka every time the cramps started. Which it did stop them, Earl has to admit. But at what cost to the babies? Or how when she started having the pains at eight and a half months, the doc gave her morphine several times rather than send her to Lexington as he should have done, given her health history, and which he finally did in a high-speed midnight ambulance ride four hours before they were born.

The doc is an old man, nearing retirement, so what would be the loss? Earl is going to kill him. He found the gun rousting an abandoned meth operation up Bee Hollow, with the numbers already filed off.

The maple tree is in the doc's back yard, maybe fifteen yards from the driveway that runs along the side of the house to the detached garage. It's a big old brick house southeast of the college, three floors and a *porte cochère*, that used to belong to Senator Oldfield. Daniels' habit, which Earl has scoped out, is to drive his car into the garage and then walk slantways from there to the back door of the house. Earl will have a clear shot and be able to get away down the alley. And he's a cop, after all. If anybody sees him in the area, they'll assume he's checking out the sound of a gunshot.

He hears the whine of tires turning in, watches the black Caddie come down the drive and slide into the garage.

And then, after two car doors slam instead of one, the doc and his wife Annie come into view. Annie is a friend of Brenda's, a sweet woman who curates the Train Depot Museum and who brought the twins matching layettes. As the couple walks towards the back door, chatting companionably, Annie rubs her husband's back and leans her head against his shoulder.

Earl has to wait two hours, until it's full dark, to come down out of the tree. It's time well spent, reflecting on what a close call he's had.

Now, as he unlocked his own door so many years later, with Brenda remarried to an auctioneer in Ashland and the twins on their own and doing well in spite of everything, Earl looked down at Mr. Bojangles, who had something in his mouth.

"Drop it," Earl said, and kicked the mess, whatever it was, into the shrubbery. Home free, he thought to himself. Still standing. Whatever else people might say about him, he was a survivor.

The dead frog from Clay Creek, with five legs and a misshapen head, would be eaten by a feral cat sometime after midnight.

Meanwhile, Jimbo sat down in his recliner catty-cornered from his wife.

"What'd Earl have to say?" she asked, snipping a thread.

Home free, he thought to himself. Still standing. Whatever else people might say about him, he was a survivor.

"Not much. We might go fishing next week." Earl's gossip about Mr. Boatman rang in his skull like a gong, knocking holes in his life's work.

"I meant to come out and say hi. I don't know what's wrong with me tonight," she said. "I feel so do-less. In fact, I've been tired a lot lately." It was her first mention of it.

He would remember that moment seven months later when she got the diagnosis, and recall it again when Earl got sick the next year and was gone by the following spring. But that night, no one yet knew that Clay Creek was contaminated from the closed Poplar Flats nuclear waste facility, which had been such a financial boost for the county. And the hell of it was, Jimbo would think in years to come, Mary Jean never accepted the cause of what killed her. Hadn't her own daddy managed Poplar Flats for fifteen years, she would argue, until that funny blood ailment forced him to retire? And wasn't her daddy a good Christian man and diligent at his job, a man who would never do anything to hurt anybody? She knew exactly where her cancer came from. It was the eyeliner she'd had tattooed on her lids during that crazy trip to Atlanta with her two best friends, when they were all three feeling so beaten up by menopause and needed a fun vacation, needed to take control of their lives. That was her story, the only explanation that made sense to her, and she stuck to it till the end. ■

GREEN HERON

Secret beside the rocks that bleed Virginia
creeper, trickling vine, where sycamores
dangle their white feet into the creek—she'll come
by slowly in the cold, last light. Small queen
of the logjam, little killer, her throat
like a cut lip rusted hungry for brim,
leech, and larvae. She baits her catch
with lure: scrap of waterspun damselfly,
but she doesn't believe in you,
though soon you cannot un-see her
crossing the half-sunk sticks behind your eyes:
her mute selection, her colorless strike.

JESS QUINLAN

NEW VIRGINIA

I.
Even before the word *land* broke
over us, we smelled the pines and

cook-smoke, a continent of old
growth and distant fires, the sound

of impossible trees shifting, leaves
rolling onto their backs.

II.
The crossing: bad enough. No
telling what powers left us

to starve, no measure of
whether we fell or were pushed

or are any less stranded
now—this place festers with ghost,

goldenrod, chickory, all the dead
vegetal blaze of September,

gold rot and pokeberry bright.
We eat the fermenting fruit, grow

crazy as birds. It's just the new world,
the covenant it makes with our bodies.

JESS QUINLAN

SEEING PINK ELEPHANTS

DARIUS STEWART

Before 2016...

It's usually around seven when I wake up, when the circadian alarm announces it's time to contend with a horrifying, if somewhat obscene, morning ritual known as the DTs—or, to employ a more gentle euphemism: "seeing pink elephants." What this means is I go to the bathroom, close the door, and let the toilet lid down. Then, I just sit (idly? No.) shaking on the cold, polypropylene. My right palm cradles the clenched left fist in a pseudo stance of prayer, one comrade bending to console the other, whereas my arms and elbows tuck in like wings or else I might fly away. I chew my lip to stall its quivering, or perhaps to muffle the ghastly noises emitting from my mouth. Continuously, I wipe my nose clean with the back of my hand when a smear caught in fluorescent light becomes a makeshift mirror reflecting a face fatigued from years of addiction. A face I want to erase. Or is it the past, supposedly, I intend to bid a tearful farewell; hence, my eyes water like a tub overflowing, seeping through the floorboards, the ceiling, thick cataracts of water veining down the walls. All the while, I sit atop the hard, cold lid tapping syncopated rhythms against the floor like a prisoner found guilty of an accused crime and nervously awaits sentencing, the gavel hammering down the verdict, the clang of gates securing him inside a cell—which is to say, at thirty-six-years-old, the one tragic flaw that has befallen several generations of Stewart men has shackled me as well.

At this hour, I should be preparing to leave the house for my job as a bartender at a local award-winning seafood house. You'd think I rise early to tend to the ordinary checklist of things-to-do: perform my daily constitutional, walk the dog so he can perform his too, take a shower, iron my uniform—white full-length bib apron with the least amount of ink stains, white dress shirt with a permanently stiff collar, pair of khakis (preferably with a side pocket on the pant leg for my cell phone), a necktie I won't mind if it's ruined from *attention please: server collisions may result in catastrophic spills when not watching (looking left while walking right) where the fuck you're going, or: piling too many dishes after bussing tables run the risk of dripping plate juices all over yourself, but worse, the floor. Translation: stupid idea. Someone (most likely, and costlier, a guest) could slip and fall, sue the place, then there'd be no reason for anyone to get out of bed at all.*

At this hour, I'm always agitated. Soon, eight o' clock will bring with it the rattling of the grim reaper's bones as he approaches with his outstretched arm, pointed finger initiating the vague sense of rigor mortis, wherein, I submit to an imagined existential crisis subjecting me to being the only surviving member of the family and, unless I procreate a child, the bloodline will die with me. The only solution to persevere agaisnt such a crisis—imagined or otherwise—is to continue murdering myself more deliberately. Translation: I need a drink, and I'm not talking "hair of the dog," but "the drink that brings back your soul."

■■■

(Someone once said that, and I have to paraphrase, "we don't want to live longer; we want to die more often." Or something like that.)

■■■

I never want to die; but each morning I wake thinking, *Today, I just might*. This is why I'm compelled to climb the stairs on legs flimsy as kite string, which means I'm inches from becoming a spool of thread on the staircase. Nevertheless, I arrive intact to the top, entering the kitchen where I store the liquor underneath the sink. But there's nothing of value there; just empty bottles of plastic; no, they're dead soldiers lined in a row like headstones; wait . . . dominoes toppling haphazardly as I scavenge for bottles containing at least a promising nip trapped in the corners that, once titled toward my open mouth, would bequeath me a tease of liquor to tide me over until I got to work. Translation: behind the bar.

I'm not without other options. A.) I could make the 20-minute journey, round-trip, to the liquor store (which opened at eight); or B.) I can take my chances at the possibility there'll be enough vodka from these near-empty bottles to percolate into my mouth. I go with option B, which requires me to stand the bottles end to end on the countertop, snake them into rows when I run out of room lengthwise. However, as I place the last bottle in the last available space, next to a corrugated bread knife, the heretofore unknown option C presents itself—and one, mind you, that's a miraculous opportunity for ingenuity: if I use the knife to cut closer to the base of each bottle, forming a lip where the liquor rests just shy of the considerably lowered brim, I can pour more out, wasting little.

I never want to die; but each morning I wake thinking, Today, I just might.

Minding my fingers, I enact this plan and manage to procure little more than a double shot of vodka that my tongue eagerly savors before I swallow it warm down my throat. This may not seem like much, but already I can feel my muscles encouraged to be still. And, despite such tenacious subterfuge, I still have time to ready myself for work. Content in the slow but certain abatement, I have newfound energy and am quite nimble descending the stairs to my bedroom where I begin dressing, humming *Thank you for being a friend* when the nine o' clock episode of *The Golden Girls* comes on. Quickly: pants pull up, belt is looped and fastened, shirt buttons and tucks, necktie is loosely affixed, but where are my shoes? Apron is folded, ready to be placed in the messenger bag, lest I forget it at home.

Then I stop. Something prevents me from putting the apron neatly at the bottom of the bag.

Q: What is it?

A: A gloriously gleaming bottle of vodka. And I do mean it shines!

I pull it out and press it to my chest, hearing its *glug glug* sing so sweetly I almost begin to harmonize with it. I crack the seal, remove the cap and chug hard. It's surprisingly chilled. I chug again and again until I can hold the bottle steady, until my outstretched hand remains parallel to the floor without trembling.

My mission is accomplished, but now I'm running late.

Quickly: slip on shoes (hiding beneath bed), sling bag over shoulder, pet dog bye, dash out door, down hill of backyard to bus stop.

The bottle may have banged a bruise by the feel of my hip, but I don't care. I've made it just in time. I reach inside the bag, tempted, as cars pass by in frequent succession, to steal a long sip. But I wait; there's no protection me from being seen on the corner tilting back at 9:30 in the morning. I settle for run fingers across the raised letters branded on the bottle until I see the shape of the bus rounding the curve in the distance. I gather my fare when it pulls to the curb and the doors open. I'm humming *Soon and very soon* ... an old hymn I learned as a child in church when we sang our prayers of thanks and contrition. I board the bus and pay the fare, still humming; and the bottle accompanies, *glug glug*, as I take my seat. ■

THE MEMORIAL

The road devours the trees and the mountain, like fruit,
excretes the miracle of convenience. At the end of the trail

a memorial looks over the valley, where mountains
crash into a shoreline of silvery pastures shot through

with pink evening light, where factories ride the fog
like freighters on a becalmed estuary. Above, the marble

memorial gleams so white the war seems to have ended
just a year or two ago though the tarnished plaques

gives the dates of two world wars. Nearby
some teenagers are drinking and having a picnic.

I didn't hike up the mountain to judge the happiness
of children watching the sunset on a wool blanket

laden with bread and beer. I came to breathe,
a necessity simpler and truer than faith, to feast

at the common table of trees and mountains.
I came to memorialize a tiny patch of earth elsewhere

whose pastures, ashes, birches, and persimmon trees
have no marble to sanctify or save,

no monument but the common one of breath.

KATHERINE SMITH

PITTSBURGH

When the word slipped from my lips,
your eyes hardened, balked

at something you did not understand.
But green, so green, my tongue labored,

and with rivers no longer ablaze. Still,
you shrugged and spoke of something

new. How grand it must be to shirk off
the cords of place and craft an identity

from metro stops and museums. Me, my
blood is thick with bituminous deposits

and halushki, of grey heartlines, one
generation removes the mother tongue,

a soul built from Stanislaus and
Czestochowa, carved into the Allegheny

Mountains, rushing with the Monongahela
River, exploding with Zambelli fireworks,

my kingdom forged from steel mills.
Mind the coming of my armies, for

ten thousand bridges guard my heritage, a
thing you might never understand

because every time you speak of my
heart, you name it *Philadelphia*, and I

know you care nothing for the Appalachian
citadel at the edge of the western gate.

SAMANTHA DEFLITCH

THE FULLBACK

ELIZABETH GENOVISE

He is an eclipse. He is divine intervention. He is the fullback. Like a vessel launched from a bed of flames sent spearing into an unsuspecting sky, he tears into the fabric of space and opens a passageway for the lone man behind him. The crazed din of the crowd and the burn of their eyes is nothing to him. Only when his brother lands in the end zone, utterly untouched, does he bend over to hold his knees and breathe. He watches Roan's familiar moonwalk and smiles faintly through the strands of hair that have fallen into his face beneath his helmet. The game, one of the last in a long line the two brothers have won for this team, is over.

Local news reporters swarm them alongside a throng of parents and classmates as they struggle to exit the field. They address only Raif: "Anything to say about the Texas rumors circulating? Anything you want to say about next year, Raif? Have you heard by any chance from the University of Tennessee?" But Raif, holding his brother's arm, maneuvers them through the mass to the safety of the locker room. There, amidst the chaos of their teammates' celebrations, Roan says into Raif's ear, "You can tell them, Raif. It's okay."

But Raif shakes his head. "None of their business," he responds.

"You can still change your mind." Then, his voice loud and strained, "I can handle it. I can hold it together by myself."

"Maybe you can," Raif says. Someone gives him a congratulatory shove and he shoves back without looking to see who it is. "But I can't let you."

■ ■ ■

They'd come into the world minutes apart. Their father, Carmichael, was absent, on a bender. Their mother, too poor to visit the clinic until she was halfway through her contractions, shocked the staff by birthing three boys in a row. The first was blue, suffocated in the birth canal, when he emerged and a nurse swiftly removed him from the room so that the young mother would not see. Next was Raif who barreled out of the womb and delighted the doctor with his exuberant screaming. Tiny Roan slid out just behind Raif, and the staff celebrated as this third child began weakly crying.

Roan tailed behind Raif all through school, relying on Raif's tutoring and constant encouragement. He was too small for his age and he was slow; more than one teacher had hinted that he ought to be put in special classes. Something was wrong with the way he saw letters on the page and for years Raif read all of their assignments out loud to him. When they discovered in middle school their talent for football, Raif taught Roan his own private reading class in a mad effort to keep his brother from having to repeat a grade. And when they started high school together, Raif did the academic work of two when he was not clearing the field for Roan. The newspapers started off by making fun of the two of them—Big R and Little R. Somebody wrote that Raif might as well be taking Roan down the field in a Radio Flyer wagon. But the coach saw them for what they were, and the two of them began to take charge of games. It turned out that there was no field Raif could not open for Roan. Roan, skinny and prone to injury, could catch anything as long as no one touched him.

Their mother had died of an overdose when they were sixteen; their father had vanished several years earlier. The boys' aunt was supposed to be living with them while they were underage, but she kept only a duffel bag at the house, and spent the nights at her boyfriend's trailer down in Holston Park on the other side of the tracks. When the twins turned eighteen she stopped coming around entirely. The old property, a small house perched on the eroding summit of a low mountain on the outskirts of Canton, was in the boys' keeping. Their thought was that if they could play college ball together, they could leave the place forever. It was understood that there was no other way they could afford college, or any other kind of escape. Neither had ever left Tennessee. Both had worked like grown men since they were fifteen. But when a scout from Texas finally came to a game, he showed interest only in Raif. "Let's face it," he said to him, "It's always been you. He's not special without you running in front of him. Look at the size of him. It's a miracle he does what he does. You can't take him with you." Then, "Look, son. You're in Canton, Tennessee. You aren't going to see a parade of scouts out here after I leave. People don't come to Canton."

"They came," Raif pointed out, gesturing at the school's stadium. "Did you see how many watched the game? They bring Channel Nine out here."

"They came to see you. This town wouldn't sell a lousy hot dog from the concession stand without you on the team."

Presented at last with an actual offer, Raif said firmly, "It's both of us or neither of us."

The response to this was disbelief followed by laughter and a repeated offer. Raif repeated himself as well and the meeting ended abruptly, both of them confused and discomfited and profoundly disappointed. The agent did not know how to explain to Raif that he was throwing away his entire life. Raif did not know how to explain to the agent that his life was not entirely his.

■ ■ ■

In the morning, Roan is slow to wake, but Raif is up and dressed by six as he is most mornings these days. Waking up early in his tiny bedroom with its low ceiling and fogged window, Raif always finds himself desperate for air. The vastness of the football field is already too far behind him and he is panicky without it.

He walks through their cluttered kitchen past piles of laundry on the breakfast table and lets the front door slap shut behind him as he steps into the late October air. For a moment he stands still on the porch. He feels, as he always does, like the captain of some battered ship caught on a rock among unforgiving waves. The house stands on a narrow plateau and the land slopes steeply downward on all sides so that there is nowhere to really walk besides the dragged gravel driveway and the tiny vegetable garden they have kept alive on the east side of the house. Higher mountains surround them, close enough that their trees block the horizon line, but too far away to alleviate the feeling of shipwreck. The land has been steadily eroding since before Raif's time and each year he and Roan have to drag more logs to the perimeter to keep the forces of nature at bay. Filling the little ravines around the house is third-growth forest thick with vines and a heavy understory that in summer is choked with mosquitoes and horseflies. Far below the house on the west side is the dry bed of an old stream, and when Raif and Roan were small, they hunted for fossils and arrowheads down there. It was an excuse to get away from the house for long periods of time, particularly on the nights their father was on a tear, zigzagging into the house drunk and furious at someone or something the twins had never met.

He dreams of massive swaths of open land, clean forest floors beneath old hardwoods, deep creeks cutting through meadows.

Raif checks on the chickens housed in a cage close to Roan's bedroom wall and discovers three small brown eggs. The first is broken but he makes a mental note of the other two. Briefly he stands on tiptoe to catch a glimpse of Roan who is sleeping smashed up against his curtainless window. Then he continues his walk to the woods' edge. The early morning mist parts around him as he starts the difficult climb down to the stream bed. He hates this land, hates its rocky slopes, his own inability to simply run here. He hates having to reach out for branches to support himself as he works his way into the wooded ravine. The land originally belonged to a man he never met—his mother's first husband who also vanished—and he has never stopped wondering why anyone would put his money into land like this, or why his mother would stay on it, building memories on a foundation of rot and ugliness. He dreams of massive swaths of open land, clean forest floors beneath old hardwoods, deep creeks cutting through meadows. Enormous beds of grass beneath fruit trees and fawns curled up in willows. A visible horizon.

His left ankle, weak from an old injury, turns a little as he loses balance, and he swears violently under his breath. He stumbles the last few feet down to the stream bed, catches himself, and holds up two middle fingers at the surrounding woods. This, too, is part of his morning walk: cursing the land when Roan can't hear.

He steps into the stream bed and begins following it in the growing light. His feet crush weak rock and in a few minutes he is at their property line—a natural clearing beneath the only pines they own. The ground is abruptly soft and the hollow echoes under Raif's shoes are a relief to him. An enormous walnut log rests in the center of the clearing, and behind it, hidden from view, is the grave of Raif and Roan's brother. Raif circles the log and eases himself down on one knee beside the flat headstone. Raif Daniels. No date. As a child, Raif had asked his mother to explain why he and his brother had the same name. His mother was high that night but Raif didn't know that at the time. "Because that's who he was supposed to be," she'd said to him, putting out her cigarette in a coffee cup. "He was supposed to be Raif. You done stole his spot."

Raif clears dirt and fallen pine needles away from the plain stone. He does the same to the walnut log. He loves this log, cherishes it even as he despises every last pebble of the rest of the land they own. Not long after the conversation with his mother about his name, he came down here in search of his brother and spotted Roan before Roan spotted him. Roan had a Walkman and a pair of headphones, things he'd gotten from a secondhand store downtown, and he was dancing wildly atop the log, holding the player high above his head. He leaped and cavorted and twisted himself in all directions and he was smiling, eyes tightly closed. Raif watched his brother until Roan wore himself out and collapsed on the grass behind the log, where the headstone was. In his happy exhaustion he seemed to have forgotten that he was lying on a grave, and Raif too forgot what lay in the ground. For just a moment, he also forgot what his mother had said to him, and his own suspicion that he did not deserve to be here. It seemed to him that he and Roan were in charge of their own fates and that he, Raif, was never meant to be anybody else but this person watching his twin dance on a log.

Now, though, the feeling seems centuries behind him. He has not seen that joyful abandon on Roan's face, or felt what he felt here, in so long. He passes his hands through his hair and finds that he is as suffocated here as he was in his bedroom. Breathless with fear. Graduation is still months away but he has no idea what they are going to do after. They don't have the money to leave but he doesn't know that he can bear to stay. Always frightened and unsure of himself off the football field, Roan has not had the courage to ask Raif about his plans since he turned down Texas. Raif badly wants to comfort his brother, but what is there to say? He has failed them both. And Roan's wide-eyed worry, his kicked-dog look, has begun to irk Raif to where he has come close to shouting at his brother for no reason at all, in the middle of a meal or while they're sitting on the back porch cleaning their squirrel rifles. He has been spending more and more time walking alone.

Raif picks up speed, following the stream bed beyond their property line and cutting left through more vertical woods toward the railroad tracks, passing a rusted bear trap from a generation ago, something he and Roan used to play in before a hunter caught them and terrified them with a story about a little boy getting killed inside an old cage just like it. Raif breathes deeply when he reaches flat land again—land bright with fallen leaves, wet scarlet and yellow leaves that stick to his shoes and flutter down beside him as he picks up stride. In the distance is Holston Park, the dull mosaic of trailer roofs just visible through the trees. It is where Raif imagines he and Roan will be, sooner than soon, and as if in answer to his worry, he hears a shotgun go off, followed by a cacophony of dogs barking.

The tracks are just ahead, glinting a little in the growing light. It is a freight line and it is where Raif's father boarded a car and left this place without a goodbye. Raif walks slowly on the irons, looking into the misted distance, imagining the rusted car carrying his father off into other mountains, into plains and coastal lands. There had never been a postcard or letter. If there had been, Raif would have burned it when it came anyway. He had been fervently grateful for his father's departure, furiously jealous of his father's escape. It meant no more screaming nights, no more hysteria as his father came swinging into their bedrooms, their mother screaming Carmichael get hold of yourself from behind walls. Raif no longer had to block doorways, take the brunt of his father's rage, let the man batter his wide shoulders and powerful chest so as to save his mother's pale cheeks or Roan's delicate ribcage from those thick knuckles. But it also meant that it was on Raif to make sure food got into the house and to make sure Roan made it through school. It meant that when the boys came home from practice one night to find their mother cold on the bathroom floor, it was on Raif to half-carry Roan out of the room, to perform futile CPR, to call the ambulance, to sign the papers. Worst of all, it meant that his father, as undeserving a man as Raif could imagine, had the freedom Raif dreamed of. None of it was fair.

Raif fishes in his jeans for a nickel or penny, wanting to lay it on the irons, to derail whatever rolls in next. But he leaves the coins in his pockets and turns back toward home. He wants these trains to keep running, needs to hear their rhythm in the night, to know the choice is there. That, and he has to get back to the house. He had promised Roan a victory hike up Mt. LeConte in the national park if they won last night's game, and he knows Roan is awake by now, waiting for him.

■ ■ ■

Mt. LeConte. It is their favorite form of weekend conditioning, and they have been loyal to it, orbiting its many trails like binary moons for years. Today they take the Alum Cave Trail, the most dramatic route, starting with a gentle climb along an emerald river and then switchbacking past rocky outcroppings and ancient gnarled trees. Usually, they scale the six miles and nearly three thousand feet in less than three hours. Today, though, they move slowly, as though their forty-five liter packs are crammed with stones. At the summit—the highest point in the Smokies—is the old Lodge, a log-cabin retreat for backpackers lit only by kerosene lamps and perched in a tiny cove carved out of the mountain. It is where they always stop to eat, drink, and regroup, but today it seems a universe away. Both boys are sweating in the October air after the first two miles.

The trail, always popular, is weirdly abandoned for a Sunday. It is just the two of them, Raif quietly chewing tobacco and Roan cramming Sour Patch Kids in his mouth as they walk. Roan worries aloud about the absence of other hikers and decides to blame it on the sky, which is heavy and dark with an incoming autumn storm. The high-elevation woods around them are impenetrable. They notice trailside bear scat every half mile or so, also a rarity on this trail, and it unnerves Roan. To ward off bears, he claps his hands hard and whistles at random intervals.

"Would you cut that out," Raif says at last. "I'm jumping out of my skin every time you do it."

Roan, just behind him, says, "You want a bear surprising us?"

"They're not interested in us. Relax. And why did you bring those stupid walking sticks? I've told you a million times, all they do is teach your body not to balance itself."

With a little huff, Roan stops and drops his pack. Raif watches as his brother funnels the foldable walking sticks into the side pockets. "Happy now?" Roan asks

Roan worries aloud about the absence of other hikers and decides to blame it on the sky, which is heavy and dark with an incoming autumn storm.

"Yeah. Great. Let's go. We're making really bad time."

They start up a fresh incline, puffing as they go. When it evens out, they are on a ledge, a rock wall to their right, an endless drop to the left. Raif starts across, one hand clutching the wire rope nailed into the rock wall. Seeing this, Roan clamps two hands around the wire and shuffles so close to Raif that Raif can smell the Sour Patch Kids.

"Give me some space, goddammit," Raif snaps. "Nobody's going to fall here. Nobody ever has."

"Then why are you holding the wire? I never saw you hold it before."

Raif lets go of the wire. "I wasn't."

They cross the ledge in silence. On the other side, under the cold shade of pine, Roan asks from behind, "What are we going to do, Raif?"

Raif walks on for a moment, eyes on the branches that intertwine above them, on the patches of bruised sky framed there. "I don't know."

"You have to know. You always know."

"Well, this time I don't, okay?"

"Maybe another scout will come before the season's over—"

"No one will. We live in Canton, remember? And anyway it doesn't matter. If they don't want us both, it's not an option." Even as he says it, Raif feels his throat closing up in anger. He wants to go. He wants to be done, forever, with the old house and working cashier jobs in town to pay utilities and looking at Roan's pleading, frightened face. He hikes faster, pounding his boots into the leafy earth, knocking up pebbles and bits of mud.

"Maybe we could just apply to some college together, not for football," Roan goes on. "I mean, just see where we get in."

Raif says nothing. On academics alone, Roan is not going to get into any college. On test scores, Roan will never leave Canton. But he can't say this, and so he hikes on, and with every step, he can hear more clearly the steady rhythm of the freight cars passing in the night below their house. He imagines himself flying down through the steep woods, rolling, nothing but his clothes on his back… and then standing at the irons' edge, poised to jump. The long mountain countryside whirling past him. The world, east of here—cities, bay towns, the ocean.

Roan reads his mind: "Maybe you wish you were Dad. Maybe you want to just get the hell out."

"Yeah, you know, maybe I do." The words are out before Raif can stop them, and he feels rather than hears his brother halt in his tracks behind him.

Then, in a rush, Roan has pushed past Raif, and is moving quickly up the trail.

"Where the fuck are you going?" Raif demands, starting after his brother.

Roan ignores him. He stalks on up the trail, legs pumping hard, and abruptly he swerves left into a little trailside clearing. Roan sits down hard on a log beside an old fire ring filled with rotten logs and ash. "You can go if you want to," he says, meeting Raif's eyes. "You should. You're never home anymore. You're always gone. Where do you go? You think I don't notice at night, and in the morning? You don't even look at me on the field anymore. You just run and assume I'm gonna make it, you don't even look back."

Startled, Raif also sits down. "No I don't. I'm always making sure."

"That's what you think. But I guess you think I should be the one apologizing. Because I fucked it all up, right? They didn't want me. If I'd been good enough, we'd have a ticket someplace. But we don't. Right? You're just that self-involved to be thinking that."

Raif studies his brother, the features that they share. Hazel eyes, dark hair, pale skin. Roan is compact and graceful where Raif is heavy-boned and unwieldy. With his delicate chin turned up toward Raif's, Roan looks far too young for his years, and suddenly, Raif wants to slap him and say the worst things he can think of. *You've only gotten this far because of me. The scout was right. I can't take you with me.*

He says, "All I'm thinking about is what we can do next."

"All you're thinking about is how to get rid of me. Just like Mom wanted to get rid of us, and Dad wanted to get rid of all three of us. You think Dad had the right idea?"

"Go fuck yourself, Roan."

For a long moment, they just sit there around the abandoned campsite. It is a mistake; the sweat on their backs has chilled beneath their shirts, and when a wind stirs the long-dead ashes in the fire pit, both boys shiver. An enormous cloud, moving fast, collides with what is left of the sun and broken shadows scatter over them. Resentfully, Raif says, "We'd better get going if we want to be back down before it pours. We're wasting time here."

They stand up together, then stop. There is a heavy rustling above them, the sound of rocks dislodging and falling down the trail. A chorus of low, urgent murmurs like a bear's guttural growl. The tiny hairs on Raif's neck lift. Roan grabs Raif's arm; Raif, on instinct, reaches backwards into his pack for the camping knife he always carries.

His hand freezes mid-motion. Roan also goes stock-still beside him. From around the blind turn above them comes

There is a heavy rustling above them, the sound of rocks dislodging and falling down the trail.

two men in national park uniforms, their backs to the boys, moving painstakingly backwards. They are holding up one end of a stretcher. At the other end are two more men, paramedics, their faces tilted down in an effort to watch both the rocks below their feet and the stretcher itself. On the stretcher is a canvas bag, zipped from top to bottom, the cloth moving in the wind, shaping the body within.

"Move aside," one of paramedics snaps, noticing them. "Move off the trail."

Raif and Roan step back into the trailside clearing, both of them almost falling into the fire pit. As the group moves closer they see a fifth man dragging behind the procession. He is about their age, maybe a few years older. He is deathly pale and his blond hair is filthy, falling into his face, covering his eyes. He is staggering under the weight of two sixty-five liter backpacks, one on his back, the other strapped to his front.

"Stop here," one of the park men says breathlessly. "Give it a minute."

For a moment the four carriers simply stand there, looking at no one. Then they gingerly set the stretcher down on the flat stretch of trail and crouch down beside it, just breathing. Raif can clearly see now that the body in the bag is that of another man, and he looks sharply at the hiker bringing up the rear. Sensing his gaze, the hiker lifts his head and brushes some of the hair off his forehead. His eyes, meeting Raif's, are a pale green, and in them Raif reads such exhausted despair that he takes an actual step backward. It is a desperate cry for help; it is as though he is asking Raif to wind back the clock, to make this all a dream. Their gaze holds.

"Move on ahead," one of the paramedics says to Raif. He is breathing hard. "No one was supposed to be on this trail today. We radioed that down hours ago. There should have been a notice posted at the trailhead."

"I'm sorry," Raif says. "We had no idea. We didn't see it."

"We're sorry," Roan echoes from just behind Raif. His voice is almost inaudible.

"I need to smoke." The hiker's voice startles all six of them with its suddenness. "Give me a minute, please." He pushes past all of them, moving downhill. Raif hesitates and then says to his brother, "Stay where you are."

He follows the hiker until he stops just off trail under a roof of rhododendron. He watches as the other man struggles to light a cigarette, using one hand to shield the flame from wind.

"Your brother?" he says, the words flying from his mouth. He points to the second backpack.

The hiker closes his eyes. "I'm Josiah," he says.

"Raif."

"He might as well have been," Josiah says.

"Your brother?"

"Conrad. It was hypothermia. They're telling me. But I don't know. We camped up there last night. I woke up and—he was just gone." Josiah drops the cigarette, grinds it out against a rock. "I came halfway down the mountain at dawn for help, then came back up. I had to check again to be sure. I couldn't believe it. I had his backpack and I didn't believe it. I did CPR over and over again. I think I broke his ribs."

"Christ. I'm sorry," Raif starts, but Josiah goes on, not hearing: "It could have happened in the middle of the night. Or ten minutes before I woke up. If I had just woken up—if I had just paid attention. If I had done one thing differently."

"It's not your fault."

Josiah fumbles for a second cigarette, then smashes the whole carton in his fist. "What do you know about it?"

"Nothing." Raif raises both hands. "Nothing. Can we help you in some way? We can help you all get down. Or I can get you home."

"Home. Oh, God." Josiah sits down slowly under the weight of the two packs. He drapes his limp arms over his head. "I'm going to have to tell his sister about this. His sister. Jesus, God."

Raif hovers above him. He glances uphill, spots Roan still frozen in place by the fire pit, eyes on the sky, anywhere but on the body bag. He knows he needs to get back up there. But Josiah below him is magnetic, the pull of his sorrow a gravity that Raif is powerless against. He slides down beside him and has a flash of sliding down beside his mother where she lay against the bathroom sink, her skin slate grey in the light of the single bulb above.

"You will get through this," Raif says.

Again, Josiah does not hear him: "He was all she had. You don't understand."

For a moment, Raif is terrified that Josiah is about to break into sobs. Then with a tremendous effort Josiah rises and squares his shoulders under the four straps. "I have to go," he says.

And he is gone, moving downhill, the procession having resumed their descent as well. Raif watches for the second time as the stretcher moves past him and then, shaking, he climbs back up to the little campsite. His brother is right where he left him, unmoving.

"You okay?" Raif asks.

Roan stares at the trail behind them. "Yeah."

"Did they talk to you?"

"Not really. They just—I think they needed a minute." Then, "I wish you hadn't left me there. But I'm glad you talked to that guy. He looked so . . . " His voice trails off.

Raif says, "I think that was the hardest thing any of them have ever had to do. Bringing him down like that."

Roan is blinking rapidly. "Do you think we should finish the hike? I mean—is that—"

"Yes," Raif says, starting ahead of him. "I think we should finish it."

They don't speak the rest of the way up. At the summit, when the clean scent of wind-worn pine meets them, they both breathe deeply but still hold their silence. They run into a group of young guides who have just finished bringing a string of llamas up the mountain, llamas bearing supplies for the Lodge, and talk with them for a few dazed moments about the animals. Then they follow the old traditions: they stop at the lodge's ancient pump to refill their bottles with frigid mountain water, buy two backpacker's lunches from the keeper in the log cabin dining hall, and follow a spur trail up to Cliff Tops—a massive overlook, a lighthouse of rock suspended above the Smoky Mountains, where the wind is so strong they have to sit on their backpacks to make sure they don't tumble the 6,000 feet down. They huddle beside a boulder and eat the lunch they know by heart: the summer sausage, the packet of Oreos, the bagel spread with cream cheese, the package of trail mix and the little cup of applesauce. Into the well water they filled their bottles with goes the orange Gatorade powder, the last treat in the lunch bags. Their movements are as fluid and synchronized as they are when pitching tents in the backcountry, when sprinting in tandem down the field; their hands might as well be tethered together. It all tastes like their history together, parallel lines in bread and sugar and footfalls. They eat in silence, staring out at the tumult of blue mountain waves, the fiery crests of autumn-lit slopes in the distance. The endless horizon.

At last, what they saw on the trail seems to hit Roan. He drops his lunch bag with a catch of his breath and puts his head down on Raif's shoulder as though they are little boys again, cowering in the bedroom after one of their father's explosions. Raif abandons his bagel to put his arm around his brother, who sobs silently into his jacket. He is keenly aware of his brother's breathing, the heat of his face against him. He feels a rush of gratefulness for the fact that he has made it this far with nothing to regret—even if he came into this world unfairly, his older brother having died in the act of opening the way for him. He thinks of how precious the burden of the living is, compared with the burden of the dead, for whom nothing can be done.

"We'll be okay," he says. "We'll be all right. I'll figure something out for us. I promise."

Roan nods into his sleeve.

"You hear me?" Raif picks up his voice, mirroring their coach's: "Hey. Do you hear me?"

"I hear you," Roan says.

"C'mon. Let's head down before it gets colder. We've got a lot of miles before we're back and you don't want to lock up."

Roan sits up and wipes roughly at his face. He hefts his pack back onto his shoulders, nods at his brother. He sticks his remaining Oreos in his shirt pocket. "Okay."

■ ■ ■

As they begin the climb down the mountain, they again find themselves behind the string of llamas. Their packs have been emptied and will be filled again tomorrow; they move slowly downhill, their guides speaking softly to them as they go. Raif falls into step behind the last one in the line and feels his brother's steps just behind his. He thinks of the final games they have left to play, and the life they have left to live afterward. He intends to keep moving forward first, blocking Hell, damming back the almighty God Himself if he has to. He follows the llamas down, the long caravan of his fear falling away from him. ■

FALSE BAPTISM

Rolling in from the lowlands every summer, a miasmatic mist
intent on its pleasures. Wealthy enough to have the luxury of
poor nerves, they preen and fawn over their kidneys, rheumatism,
flour albus and scrofulitic afflictions, one group even carting up
their own preacher, a softer, fawning gospel bent to please their
itching ears, his dulcet tones bathing them in nothing but easy
forgiveness, billiards and ballrooms & a wide, smooth path
instead of the narrow thicket where the one lamb resides.
They praise the pure air & mineral waters soothing their aching
joints while turning up their noses at the daughters and sons
of these healing streams who silently fill up dippers from metal
buckets as their charges rock on the veranda loosely talking.
In one pool at Catoosa I hear tell women and men convened
who were not married or even properly acquainted, flirting
& cavorting in the same fizzing wanton bubbles & in this
sickness believed they were healing themselves. Called the stench
perfume. *What was good enough for the Romans,* one lawyer winked,

paying no mind to me scrubbing the piazza, and I tell you what was
good enough for them. Ransacking Jerusalem. Crucifying our Lord.
The only man I ever talked to more than a little was a dedicated
valetudinarian from Macon who proved a skeptical Ponce de Leon,
dabbing his thin wrists with water drops every few hours,
but determined, mainly, to finish his geological treaty, thereby
sealing one last somewhat acceptable scholarly contribution.
We exchanged friendly pleasantries for awhile, but the day I
dared quote John 7:38, *He that believeth on me, as the scripture hath*
said, out of his belly shall flow rivers of living water, he held up his
pale wavering hand, rejecting our Lord for Lyell's and Hutton's
deceitful theories, slow forces laboring through long periods,
trees rocks and hills straggling along for epochs when our
Magnificent Creator changes all manner of things in the snap
of a twig on Damascus road. I have not always seen justice
come to the just, this I allow, but I have seen the old creation
fall away the very moment a man's heart finally chooses to
stoop & beg, his face still splotched & whiskey ravaged, veins

continuing to pulsate across the smashed bulbous nose but with
a countenance so transformed he might need well put a veil upon
his visage just as Moses did coming down off the Mountain,
properly shielding the wondering people from so much glory.

JENN BLAIR

MADE OUT OF WORDS

CHARLES GREEN

If you've attended a few poetry and fiction readings, you've learned to cringe at the question, "Where do you get your ideas?" Usually, student writers ask like proselytes who need one key phrase to open up their own locked vision, and the writer stares at the floor, looking for an answer. Pervasive as the question is, though, I'm no longer irritated by those who ask; I've seen so many writers flail impromptu responses that I've turned my mild ire to those writers unprepared for what they should know is coming.

Harlan Ellison's response is that he has an idea guy in Poughkeepsie. I like the idea that there stands, adjacent to IBM's campus, a warehouse of mainframes that generate ideas, ready to ship. But the only memorably good reply I've heard that actually tried to answer is Michael Chabon's, given at AWP a few years back. As summarized and simplified from my memory: ideas are everywhere, so getting them is easy. Writers can pluck any idea and, with enough attention and care, develop them into wonder.

Chabon's emphasis on patience and process echoes my own teaching, but I don't find his answer satisfying, and neither do my Intro to Creative Writing students. I don't blame him for offering a smart but unsatisfying answer; in fact, I admire him for crafting it even though he can't answer it. No writer can, because for years we've overlooked the real problem: it's the wrong question.

Consider how it's framed in its two main iterations, *where do you get your ideas* and *where do your ideas come from: where, get,* or *come from*—the language of place, as if the material for writing arrives fully formed from some specific locale, the Muse having done the irksome work down the assembly line to put together the Stanza just as autoworkers did the Nissan Stanza. If ideas come from a physical place, maybe Poughkeepsie is as good an answer as any—the name Poughkeepsie comes from the Wappinger tribe's word that means, roughly, "the reed-covered lodge by the little-water place." That sounds like a pastoral writer's cottage, a great place to get ideas.

The question's biggest misunderstanding, though, isn't the language of place: it's the word *ideas*. Are *ideas* the starting point, or even the core, of writing? Obviously, writing isn't absent ideas—writers often mention having an idea—but I think we need to re-translate the language of writing away from *ideas*, perhaps back toward the Greek origin of the word, *idein*, meaning "to see." To borrow an anecdote from David Mason and John Frederick Nims's *Western Wind*: when the painter Edgar Degas said that he couldn't write well despite being "full of ideas," Stéphane Mallarmé replied, "My dear Degas, poems are not made out of ideas. They're made out of words."

In that quote, Degas sounds too much like many undergraduate writers I've taught, and even at times like me. "I have an idea for a poem," they say, "but I just can't get it on the page." The idea of the idea serves as a kind of block. I suspect, based on my own experience, that they don't have *an* idea for a poem in their heads, but *several* ideations: the vague visual image of a poem on the page, a cluster of sensory memories, emotions named and unnamable. Students want me to tell them how to translate the idea into word, but they don't understand that moving from idea to object requires several translations: from sensory memory into language, from feeling into object, from the sense of poetic lines into the actual tensions and torsions of language.

Like all writers, they want things other than words to become words. Of course, young writers don't ask, "Where do you get your words?" Imagine Gerard Manley Hopkins behind a university lectern as a rapt audience listens. One hand rests next to the Aquafina bottle provided by the English Department. He intones into the microphone, "'No wonder of it: shéer plód makes plough down sillion/Shine, and blue-bleak embers, ah my dear,/Fall, gall themselves, and gash gold-vermillion.' Thank you for coming." Applause; the host announces time for questions. After a silence, an undergrad in the third row raises his hand. "Where," he asks (because *he* always asks the first question), "do you get your sounds?"

Where do you get your sentence structures, your lines, your line breaks?

■ ■ ■

Pushing against the question "where do you get your ideas" only gets us so far. Young writers still will ask at readings; my Intro students will ask. The question may be the wrong one, but the questions that underlie it are worth asking. And they deserve an answer to those underlying questions. When someone asks "Where do you get your ideas," I hear several questions: *What is the secret code to writing well? What am I supposed to write about, and how do I decide? Why is published writing polished while mine is a mess on the page?* The anxiety that nudges forward the question comes from a directive need: *inspire me.* I know that feeling well, the desire for the Great Writer's aura to spread to and blanket you. The anxiety, like most, begs for certainty, for reassurance, but writing isn't about either of those. In his essay "Not-Knowing," Donald Barthelme clarifies that certainty is impossible (admittedly, *clarifies* is ironic in this context): "It's appropriate to pause and say that the writer is one who, embarking upon a task, does not know what to do." Uncertainty animates the process. When we write—and, to be clear, I mean writing that takes as its mantra Robert Frost's "No surprise for the writer, no surprise for the reader"—we have to live in a dark room and give shape to that space. We may whisper portentously and pretentiously in our heads, "I go to encounter for the millionth time the reality of experience and to forge in the smithy of my soul the uncreated conscience of my race," but that whisper doesn't tell us how.

We can take those anxious questions further, as close to the root as we can. *Why do you write? How did you know or decide you were a writer? Am I a writer?* (Yes, we can peel these questions down to the root bulb of existential dread: *Why am I alive? Does this life have meaning? How can I invest this life with meaning?* But I don't think I need to address those here, mainly because I don't even rise to the level of armchair philosopher. I am, at best, a folding-chair philosopher, and that folding chair has been left in the backyard to gather pine needles and leaves in its seat.)

I'd like to reframe these questions, maybe arbitrarily, into the following: *What motivates you to write?* If this were a film, the writer (as always in films, a bearded man) would respond, "What motivates *you* to write?" A string quartet would underscore the moment; later in the film, a montage would

I'd like to reframe these questions, maybe arbitrarily, into the following: What motivates you to write?

show the young students—all male, most likely—in the woods, *Inspired* as they rip the front pages from their pedantic poetry textbooks. One, wearing his school jacket inside-out, shouts, "Our verse shall be Free!"

The question of motivation isn't an arbitrary choice. Writers must choose to write. Many writers say they have no choice, that they simply have to write, but to pursue a piece of writing to completion is still a choice. Ultimately, because motivation can be so individual and our choices dictated at times by impulses we don't even notice, let alone articulate, each writer can answer differently, describing her own experience and generalizing from that. For example, during breaks in graduate school, I would drive from Columbia,

Missouri, to Maumelle, Arkansas, and back. I regularly passed a road sign for Snowball, Arkansas, an unincorporated community I'd never heard of and have still never visited. The name made me laugh; a fantasy about outsiders in that place rattled in my head; and the words and images nagged me through the start of writing, all the way, as luck would have it, to publication.

Different things motivate me on different days, of course—*things* being a technical term for sensory images, wordplay, memories and their misremembered cousins, the varieties of matter my various senses have compiled along axons in my brain, material waiting to be kicked up by a passing synapse. And, more importantly, my fantasy answer of "What motivates *you* to write" isn't instructive, either, at least not concretely so. The audience and my students, they want direction. At one level, the answer is: if you are motivated, then write. Toni Morrison advises young writers, "If there's a book that you want to read, but it hasn't been written yet, then you must write it"; in his poem "Two Tramps in Mud Time," Robert Frost writes, "My object in living is to unite / My avocation and my vocation / As my two eyes make one in sight." Both suggest a *must*, an *object*, a goal.

But motivation is only part of what young writers want. I also hear cloaked inside "where do you get your ideas" this anxiety: "My head is full of lightning bugs; which ones should I enclose in a jar to show people?" In other words, "How do you decide what to write?"

One answer, which extends from the old adage, frayed as a decade-old coir doormat, is to write what you know. Of course, our knowledge of our own knowledge is tenuous; hence Flannery O'Connor's "I write to discover what I know." In *Making Shapely Fiction*, Jerome Stern inverts the advice to "don't write what you don't know." I'd like to take it a step further: Writing explores what you know and what you don't, and how you might map those territories. What I know one day may turn obsolete tomorrow.

Another answer to *how do you decide what to write,* perhaps as unhelpful as a poster of a cat hanging from a tree branch, captioned "Hang in there!": you just write. For example, as an undergraduate, I sat in my poetry teacher Ralph Burns's office and said, "I don't know what to write about." Behind his big glasses, he looked at me a moment, and for a moment I saw into the core of disdain. By chance, in the next office, someone guffawed.

Ralph asked, "What did that sound like to you?"

What came to me immediately: "Like someone falling down the stairs."

"Write that down."

I did. He told me to keep writing. I did so, in and beyond his office, and I crafted that line into part of a poem that I finished for that undergrad workshop, a poem that felt like a success. It's now boxed away in an air-conditioned storage unit, but without that poem, without Ralph nudging me past my fear, I wouldn't have kept writing.

Even though the advice sounds ominously close to "Just Do It," "you just do" seems close to the right answer to me. If you want to write, choose to write.

But the audience and my students want categories, vocabulary, a quote that resides in their minds as a reminder. They may misremember, misuse, or misquote later, as I have with my teachers, but they want those. We can craft figures and analogize, like so: In her wonderful personal essay "The Pain Scale," Eula Biss writes, "My father once told me that an itch is just very mild pain. Both sensations simply signal, he told me, irritated or damaged tissue." Analogously: the writer's brain is damaged tissue. (Please do not interpret "the writer's brain is damaged tissue" as reinforcing or endorsing the idea that writers and artists are mad, insane, clinical, etc. Instead, I mean that all brains, all cells, are damaged, at least in the sense that they are always in transit, from one moment to the next, searching for a permanent cure to permanent change.) That damaged tissue produces an itch. Writing scratches that itch. Sometimes it goes away, and other times it becomes a pain signaled by an ailing you didn't know you had, an ailing you have to treat with more writing.

Of course, analogies only go so far. Here is the answer I give my students, as pithy and quick as I can make it.

I'm not a religious person, but I prefer the idea of prayer as an act of discovering the extent of one's own faith. So it is, I'd like to think, with writing.

What constitutes the material of writing and answers all the questions that underlie *where do you get your ideas*: Obsessions and observations.

Here's how I define obsessions: Over years of reading and writing, I've discovered clusters of interests that have evolved over time. These interests don't need or bear categorization, but they include formal and intellectual interests in writing, from genre concerns to sentence structure to the construction of a narrative persona; emotional concerns, including various experiences of intimacy and loneliness; and ongoing curiosities that move among any categories I may make—for example, the extent to which we often justify our emotional impulses in rational language. The various interests I've listed in this paragraph are abstract and general, but they instantiate themselves in concrete, specific ways, and the writing that has responded to them has responded to concrete, specific moments.

And observations: Any image, phrase, or thought that rattles around my head long or loud enough to draw my attention, I'll write down. Anything I notice that seems even remotely noteworthy (an adult knotting a straw like it's a balloon animal, or a black splotch of gum on a hallway floor), I'll write down. If, say, a metric rhythm insists itself in my head, I'll try to fill it with words. If jotting soothes the observational itch, I move on. If the itch persists or arises again as I'm working another itch, I keep scratching.

I intend for students to interpret *obsessions and observations* as broadly as possible, but with a caveat: writing isn't (at least for me) a series of moments in which I ask, "so what are my obsessions and observations"; instead, it is an ongoing habit of mind, one I alternately trust and doubt at various points in the writing process. I'm not a religious person, but I prefer the idea of prayer as an act of discovering the extent of one's own faith. So it is, I'd like to think, with writing.

■ ■ ■

I still wonder, though, how the particular form of that question—Where do you get your ideas?—became so standard. I have several speculations, though I have little sense of how right they are. Most immediate is the common student problem of the abstract: students want to engage the reader's emotions and thoughts, but they think that to do so means they must name those. They tend to think of literature with a capital-L, of Themes like War, Love, Death, Themes as they learn in high school—Themes seem primary in their approach. However we choose to emphasize the concrete—no ideas but in things (things being a technical term, etc.); show, don't tell (or, more accurately, show as much as necessary, and tell when you have to)—we have to reorient their minds away from the abstract, away from *ideas,* toward the world as they encounter it through their own perceiving senses. The senses are limited, so I want *perceive* to resonate more fully than it does these days; I want to draw on the Latin roots, meaning to *seize entirely* and *to take possession of.* I want to convey to my students how important it is for their writing to seize entirely the world of their senses that gives them their world of ideas; I want to convey how important it is for their writing to be object, not idea.

My other speculations about the form of the question have to do with the teaching of creative writing. (Yes, I think it can be taught, and not just because my paycheck relies on it.) I've encountered many students over the years who say, sometimes in the classroom and sometimes in my office, "I'm not creative." The tone always seems either defensive or apologetic: *don't judge me too hard.* I think that tone is an unintended negative of herding the writing of poetry, fiction, and creative nonfiction within the disciplinary fence of *creative* writing. Other acts of writing are, then, uncreative, though academic writing, even at its most superficially and substantively dull, requires creativity. If a student has ever fantasized about an argument or an upcoming date, the student has been creative. We may judge such creativity as basic, but when I ask my students to describe the work they do in their (non-English) majors, they describe vitally creative processes. But I think *creative,* for students, is synonymous with *original,* and neither word comes without complications. Though my definition is neither necessary nor sufficient, I think of creativity—in writing or otherwise—as a process of oscillation between the known and unknown past, the known and unknown present, and the known and unknown future.

■ ■ ■

Another problem for young writers is one teachers of first-year essay writing have studied for decades, since the groundbreaking work of Janet Emig and Donald Murray: the difference between process and product. In creative-writing courses, we teach published writing alongside student drafts. Students who've written on keyboards and screens for most of their lives face a double tyranny: the clean pre-formatting of word processing, where an imperfect paragraph can disappear so easily, and the greatness of the writing we show them. As teachers, we can show students Anne Lamott's chapter on "Shitty First Drafts" from *Bird by Bird*, and we can quote Ernest Hemingway's direct "The first draft of anything is shit," but we can't really show students the many drafting stages of, say, Robert Hayden's "Those Winter Sundays" or, even more crucially, the years of poems he wrote and the many drafts of those, the early poems in which he learned his craft, the reading history that accreted in his imagination, the culture in which he shaped himself.

Because the Muse still holds young writers in headlocks. Many disdain discipline and wait for inspiration. Product over process. But the writer isn't Matthew in Caravaggio's "The Inspiration of St. Matthew," transcribing from the angel above in a whirl of sheets. Those of us who teach need to reinscribe *inspiration* for students: not the rare appearance of the angel to whisper the right words in the right order, but inspiration as breath: necessarily daily, from moment to moment. Not taken for granted, but bodily. Or, in secular terms adapted from an old theological debate: not faith alone, but faith and works. Let the senses inhale; write to exhale. The processes vary: craft the best sentence you can, then fill the shape of that sentence's wake, and then the next and the next until the water is still, or fill a page or ten, then pare and shape and edge until you find the words.

■ ■ ■

Ultimately, these questions have no single answers. Student writers suffer from seeing publication as the reward, so they need some reassurance that they aren't wasting their time. That's why the question keeps getting asked; that's why writers flail and demure and craft figures in response. Novice or Nobel Laureate, each writer has to write her own answers. For now, I'm just going to keep plugging away, obsessing and observing, mapping the territories of what I know and what I don't, each day trying to draw lines so I can incorporate my own Poughkeepsie. ■

GRANDPA JIMMY'S LESSONS

how the body
is like an acoustic guitar
strings the texture of your daughter's
hair, your fingers clasped
over her small open mouth
strumming a muffled sob

you taught the sound
of a body is not always beautiful
the same way God lives in a double barrel
shotgun if you look at it just right
and how to put a man down with a bottle
just as easy as a baby

SOSHA PINSON

CHASING BREAD

SADIE SHORR-PARKS

For breakfast, we ate old cheese with the polka-dots cut off and drank the red tea you brought back from Cape Town. I handed you slices of cheese in silence as we sat on our beloved Oriental rug. I suggested we paint our walls the color of our tea-stained mugs.

For lunch, we felt too lively to eat our ham. We wished for kale and ginger, a house whose walls weren't shedding—maybe the curved yellow kind in Paris, or the flat brown types in Brooklyn. We scribbled our plans on legal pads and picked at our toes.

For dinner, we slurped soup and sucked down wine. We went to our deck, watched bats punctuate the pink sky. You painted your nails to match the holly bush and I applied my blush to match the bats. We looked at our long lawn for more inspiration; we spit out fruit seeds; we retreated indoors having gathered nothing but bug bites. ■

A DEFINITION OF DOMINION

On the curve of pasture, concrete stairs
are a grey memorial of the stolen house.
Two trees loiter in their restless shade
distracted by birds, are unaware
of absence. Cows nuzzle them.
Field mice fill the bleachers to a mouse
cheering some contest of fables.
The risers add up to nothing—
nothing but storm-starved clouds
skimming the blue where gables
should be, except the invisible trails
of crows who see no landing;
no chimney draws them, now
rubble ready for copperheads.
Do not ask Time to mend what fails
memory or ask fire to repent.
            You *can* wonder how
a petal of painted porcelain has settled,
pleadingly white on the highest altar
and what is it that is meant.
As around any lettered stone, dark
earth rises, reversing the welcome,
erasing the domestic curse.
The lowest tread now tread upon
by the roots of thistle and jimson weed,
spiders and worms become
indifferent neighbors in their own need.

FREDERICK WILBUR

BOOK REVIEW

Erik Reece. *Utopia Drive: A Road Trip Through America's Most Radical Idea*. New York, NY: Farrar, Straus and Giroux, 2016. 368 pages. Hardcover. $28.00.

Reviewed by Jayne Moore Waldrop

Utopia Drive: A Road Trip Through America's Most Radical Idea by Erik Reece provides an opportunity to step away from current fractious political discourse and explore unique attempts—past and present—at crafting the ideal society.

During a period of personal comfort that included a new marriage, a job teaching creative writing at the University of Kentucky, and a creekside cabin in the woods, Reece couldn't ignore his nagging worry about the nation's growing income inequality, erosion of public trust, and rampant consumption of material goods. Setting out to look for answers rooted in past intellectual traditions and perhaps find inspiration for the future, Reece charted a road trip to several utopian communities in the eastern United States that flourished in the 1800s as well as present-day egalitarian sites.

For anyone who has read Reece's previous work, his search for answers will come as no surprise. In his first book, *Lost Mountain: A Year in the Vanishing Wilderness, Radical Strip Mining and the Devastation of Appalachia*, Reece wrote a modern-day call to arms about strip mining by chronicling a year he spent as witness to the systematic destruction of a single mountain. Clearly, Reece is willing to get personal with radical ideas and in doing so, he gives form to the forces of change.

In *Utopia Drive*, Reece makes his first stop at a Shaker community with a most idyllic sounding name—Pleasant Hill—a mere sixteen miles from the author's home in Nonesuch, Kentucky. The Shakers laid the cornerstone for the settlement in 1809 during a time when the Kentucky wilderness was a hub for the religious fervor of the country's Second Great Awakening. Unlike most groups of the era, the Shakers were radically progressive on gender and racial equality. Each community had both a spiritual mother and father. They welcomed as equals freed slaves who joined them. Reece describes fully the simple beauty of the place from its architecture to its current focus on sustainable farming.

He travels on to places founded outside mainstream culture, including the Abbey of Our Lady of Gethsemani; New Harmony, Indiana; Modern Times on Long Island, New York, and Thoreau's Walden Pond. While those who established utopian communities differed in their goals—whether religious, economic or political—they all dared to imagine markedly different American dreams.

Along the journey Reece reveals a great deal about himself, expanding the book to include aspects of memoir.

In downtown Cincinnati he looks for Josiah Warren's first cooperative general store, an enterprise based on Warren's economic theory of equitable commerce. While in town, Reece heads to the baseball stadium to catch part of a Reds game. A passage about his relationship with his stepfather is particularly poignant in the context of their mutual love of the Cincinnati Reds, Pete Rose, and the team's glory days when Reece was a kid. He also connects the former co-op site to the present location of Duke Energy Convention Center, linking the spot to the great wealth of James Duke, his empire built on tobacco and coal, and eventually to Duke University basketball, about which Reece acknowledges feelings that are "complex and perhaps at times irrational."

Clearly, Reece is willing to get personal with radical ideas and in doing so, he gives form to the forces of change.

Reece pays tribute to the relatively unknown Warren as creator of the cooperative, one of the country's most progressive notions. A refugee of the utopian efforts at New Harmony, Warren saw that community's failings and formulated his own ideas of economic and social reformation. He respected the sovereignty of the individual while valuing the benefits of voluntary cooperation in the mutual interest of all parties.

> *Warren proposed...a single economic mandate he called 'equitable commerce'....Warren stipulated that price should not be determined by the value of something to a buyer, but rather by the cost of producing it, measured in time, exertion, and materials. A man dying of thirst, after all, will give everything he owns for a glass of*

water—that is its value to him at the moment—but only a scoundrel would charge or accept such a price. Yet this logic that value should determine price is, to varying degrees, the basis of modern capitalism.

Warren also believed that access to an egalitarian media went hand-in-hand with social change, a concept surely endorsed by modern grassroots organizations who organize via social media. He recognized that mainstream media of his day failed to promote novel ideas like his theories of cooperative individualism. In response, he invented the country's first continuous-feed rotary press that could provide an inexpensive and accessible flow of information. The ability to freely promote ideas was so important to Warren that he gave his invention to the public without securing a patent.

Further down the road, Reece experiences life at modern-day egalitarian communities in Louisa County, Virginia. He stays for a few days at Twin Oaks, a thriving community founded in 1967, where he picks cucumbers in exchange for room and board. He describes its residents, governance and beauty, as well as its shortcomings. And as the mileage increases along the drive, Reece discovers a lot about himself.

I'm too tight-assed to become a nudist. I'm too much of an introvert, too ill-suited for the relentless socialness of these admirable communities. I want to be left alone to read and write and to wander the woods around my house. I belong too much to my own utopia of solitude that consists of me, my wife, my dogs, and a few dependable neighbors. Here in the utopia of solidarity, I fear I would yearn for that isolation.

Reece's conversational writing style makes the rich lessons in history and economics feel fresh and current. His ability to bridge historical research to contemporary culture engages the reader and gives context for why it all matters. The book is an accomplishment, a confluence of economic theory, environmental concerns, spirituality, human nature, and the American dream in its many forms, perfectly timed for broadening the national conversation on how to create a more perfect union. ■

WINTER NIGHT SOLSTICE

Quarter moon converses with clouds
in symposium aloft, musing, casually floating ideas,
adrift in thought, passing off bon mots,
with subtle nuance, obscure allusions,
something elliptic, something recondite
and something of hope.

Cryptic remarks emerge and onward ride
in open delight, of dreams long held,
then lightly veiled in half-tone threads of
unfinished aspirations.

Memories swiftly rise, headlong
tumble into tints of amber, blue and grey—gather,
glare and fade when a sailing buzzard of blackness holds
    sway—
holds long enough just to say:
even this will pass.

So onward goes the discourse,
with subtlety, brilliance,
gentle wit, ever the matchless woman holds sway
in timeless symposium of dear, familiar,
ever nimble clouds.

BR. PAUL QUENON

CONTRIBUTORS

Jenn Blair's work has appeared or is forthcoming in *The Chattahoochee Review, New South, Copper Nickel, South Carolina Review, Pembroke Magazine, Rattle, Berkley Poetry Review,* the *James Dickey Review,* and *Cold Mountain Review,* among others. Her poetry manuscript *Malcontent* is forthcoming from Press Americana. She lives in Winterville, Georgia.

Samantha DeFlitch is a native of the Laurel Highlands surrounding Pittsburgh, Pennsylvania. She is a graduate of the College of William and Mary, and is currently attending the University of New Hampshire in pursuit of her MFA.

Elizabeth Genovise's fiction has appeared in *Cimarron Review, The Southern Review, Cold Mountain Review, Pembroke Magazine,* and other journals. She has published two collections of short stories, *A Different Harbor* and *Where There Are Two or More,* and is the recipient of a 2016 O. Henry Prize.

Denise Giardina is the author of six novels, including the national bestsellers *Storming Heaven, The Unquiet Earth,* and most recently, *Emily's Ghost.* She lives in Charleston, West Virginia.

Robert Gipe is the author of *Trampoline,* winner of the 2016 Weatherford Award in Fiction. He lives in Harlan, Kentucky, and grew up in Kingsport, Tennessee. His fiction has appeared in *Appalachian Heritage, Still, Motif,* and *Pine Mountain Sand & Gravel.*

Originally from Arkansas, **Charles Green** lives in Cortland, New York. His writing has appeared or is forthcoming in T*he Southeast Review, Fiction International,* and *The New England Review,* among other venues. He teaches writing at Cornell University.

Ron Houchin has work recently in or forthcoming in *The Galway Review, Devil Fish Review, Potomac Review, Birmingham Poetry Review,* and *Blue Lyra Review.* His eighth book of poetry, *Planet of the Best Love Songs,* is due out in Spring 2017 from Salmon Publishing of Ireland. Next May will mark his twenty-seventh visit to Ireland.

Elaine Fowler Palencia, now of Champaign, Illinois, grew up in Morehead, Kentucky. She is the author of three poetry chapbooks, including *Going Places*, and two collections of Appalachian short stories, *Small Caucasian Woman* and *Brier Country*.

Sadie Shorr-Parks is a poet and essayist from Philadelphia. She currently a lecturer at Shepherd University. Her writing has appeared in *Blueline, Defunct Magazine*, and *Sierra Nevada Review*, among others. Her book reviews have been published by *Iowa Review* and *Southern Literary Review*.

Sosha Pinson is a poet originally from Pikeville, Kentucky. She received her MFA in Poetry from Drew University and her BFA in Creative Writing from Morehead State University. Her poems can be found in *Circe's Lament: Anthology of Wild Women Poetry, Minerva Rising, The Wide Shore*, and *Still: The Journal*, among others.

Born in West Virginia, **Br. Paul Quenon**, OCSO entered the Trappists in 1958 at the Abbey of Gethsemani in Kentucky, where Thomas Merton was his Novice Master. He has been publishing poems and photographs for the last twenty years. Quenon's latest books of poetry are *Unquiet Vigil* and *Bells of the Hours*.

Jess Quinlan is a poet and essayist writing in the Shenandoah Valley. She was trained out of the Hollins University MFA program. Her work dwells in the landscapes and people of her native Virginia, seeking purpose in the live wire of history that still smokes in those spaces. Recently, she was the recipient of the Graybeal-Gowen Prize for Virginia Poets.

Katherine Smith's poems have appeared in a number of journals, among them *The Cincinnati Review, Ploughshares, Mezzo Cammin, Shenandoah, The Southern Review, Atlanta Review*, and *Appalachian Heritage*. Her first book, *Argument by Design*, appeared in 2003. Her second book of poetry, *Woman Alone on the Mountain*, appeared with Iris Press in Fall 2014. She teaches at Montgomery College in Maryland where she is Poetry Editor for the *Potomac Review*.

Darius Stewart is the author of three chapbook collections of poetry: *The Terribly Beautiful* (2006), *Sotto Voce* (2008), and *The Ghost the*

Night Becomes (2014, winner of the 2013 Gertrude Press Poetry Chapbook Prize). His work also appears in anthologies and national journals of the literary arts. He resides in Knoxville, Tennessee, somewhat peacefully, with his dog, Fry.

Ida Stewart is the author of *Gloss,* winner of the 2011 Perugia Press Prize. Her poems can also be found in journals including *Field,* the *Laurel Review,* the *Tusculum Review,* and *Connotation Press.* She holds an MFA in creative writing from the Ohio State University and a PhD in English from the University of Georgia. A native of West Virginia, she currently lives in Philadelphia and teaches writing at the University of Delaware.

Kopana Terry works in many mediums: photography, music, drawing, writing, and on occasion, radio. Her blog, the outhouse: where art goes (www.kopana.net/the-outhouse), combines art with positive thought. When she's not creating art, Terry is the Oral History Archivist, Historical Newspaper Curator, and Library Manager at the University of Kentucky Louis B. Nunn Center for Oral History.

Jayne Moore Waldrop is a Lexington writer and attorney. Her work has appeared or is forthcoming in *New Madrid Journal, Kudzu, Luna Station Quarterly, Deep South, Limestone Journal, Minerva Rising* ,and *Kentucky Monthly* magazine. A contributing columnist for the Louisville *Courier-Journal,* she writes a monthly column about Kentucky books and authors.

Frederick Wilbur's poems have appeared in *Shenandoah, Green Mountains Review, The Lyric, The South Carolina Review, Cold Mountain Review, The Greensboro Review, Hampden-Sydney Poetry Review, New Virginia Review,* and *Southern Poetry Review.* He is an architectural woodcarver and has authored three dozen articles and three books on the subject. He lives in the Blue Ridge Mountains of central Virginia.